NYSTCE 022

English to Speakers of Other Languages
Teacher Certification Exam

By: Sharon Wynne, M.S.
Southern Connecticut State University

"And, while there's no reason yet to panic, I think it's only prudent that we make preparations to panic."

XAMonline, INC.
Boston

Library of Congress Cataloging-in-Publication Data

Wynne, Sharon A.
NYSTCE English to Speakers of Other Languages 022: Teacher Certification / Sharon A. Wynne.
1st ed. ISBN 978-1-60787- 153-8
1. NYSTCE English to Speakers of Other Languages 022   2. Study Guides.
3. NYSTCE   4. Teachers' Certification & Licensure.   5. Careers

Disclaimer:

The opinions expressed in this publication are the sole works of XAMonline and were created independently from the National Education Association, Educational Testing Service, or any State Department of Education, National Evaluation Systems or other testing affiliates.

Between the time of publication and printing, state specific standards as well as testing formats and website information may change that is not included in part or in whole within this product. Sample test questions are developed by XAMonline and reflect similar content as on real tests; however, they are not former tests. XAMonline assembles content that aligns with state standards but makes no claims nor guarantees teacher candidates a passing score. Numerical scores are determined by testing companies such as NES or ETS and then are compared with individual state standards. A passing score varies from state to state.

Printed in the United States of America

NYSTCE English to Speakers of Other Languages 022
ISBN: 978-1-60787-153-8

About XAMonline

Founded in 1996, XAMonline began with one teacher-in-training who was frustrated by the lack of materials available for certification exam preparation. From a single state-specific guide, XAMonline has grown to offer guides for every state exam, as well as the PRAXIS series.

Each study guide offers more than just the competencies and skills required to pass the test. The core text material leads the teacher beyond rote memorization of skills to mastery of subject matter, a necessary step for effective teaching. XAMonline's unique publishing model brings currency and innovation to teacher preparation.

- Print-on-demand technology allows for the most up-to-date guides that are first to market when tests change or are updated.

- The highest quality standards are maintained by using seasoned, professional teachers who are experts in their field to author the guides.

- Each guide includes varied levels of vigor in a comprehensive practice test so that the study experience closely matches the actual in-test experience.

- The content of the guides is relevant and engaging.

At its inception, XAMonline was a forward-thinking company, and we remain committed to bring new ways of studying and learning to the teaching profession. We choose from a pool of over 1500 certified teachers to review, edit, and write our guides. We partner with technology firms to bring innovation to study habits, offering online test functionality, a personalized flash card builder, and ebooks that allow teachers in training to make personal notes, highlight, and study the material in a variety of ways.

To date XAMonline has helped nearly 500,000 teachers pass their certification or licensing exam. Our commitment to preparation exceeds the expectation of simply providing the proper material for study; it extends from helping teachers gain mastery of the subject matter and giving them the tools to become the most effective classroom leaders possible to ushering today's students towards a successful future.

How to Use This Book

Help! Where do I begin?

Begin at the beginning. Our informal polls show that most people begin studying up to 8 weeks prior to the test date, so start early. Then ask yourself some questions: How much do you really know? Are you coming to the test straight from your teacher-education program or are you having to review subjects you haven't considered in 10 years? Either way, take a diagnostic or assessment test first. Also, spend time on sample tests so that you become accustomed to the way the actual test will appear.

A diagnostic can help you decide how to manage your study time and reveal things about your compendium of knowledge. Although this guide is structured to follow the order of the test, you are not required to study in that order. By finding a time-management and study plan that fits your life you will be more effective. The results of your diagnostic or self-assessment test can be a guide for how to manage your time and point you towards an area that needs more attention.

You may also want to structure your study time based on the percentage of questions on the test. For example, 25% of the Mathematics questions focus on Algebraic Concepts. **Note,** this doesn't mean that it is equal to a 25% of the test's worth. Remember the distribution charts from above: each major content area is devoted an equal amount of questions, but within the content areas the number of questions per subject area varies greatly. Depending on your grasp of any one topic, you may want to devote time comparable to the number of questions. See the example study rubric below for an idea of how you might structure your study plan.

Week	Activity
8 weeks prior to test	Take a diagnostic or pre-assessment test then build your study plan accordingly to your time availability and areas that need the most work.
7 weeks prior to test	Read the entire study guide. This does not have to be an in-depth reading, but you should take the time to mark sections or areas you know you'd like to return to or can be skimmed in further study.
6-3 weeks prior to test	For each of these 4 weeks, choose a content area to study. You don't have to go in the order of the book. It may be that you start with the content that needs the most review. Alternately, you may want to ease yourself into plan by starting with the most familiar material.
2 weeks prior to test	Take the sample test, score it, and create a review plan for the final week before the test.
1 week prior to test	Following your plan (which will likely be aligned with the areas that need the most review) go back and study the sections that align with the questions you may have gotten wrong. Then go back and study the sections related to the questions you answered correctly. If need be, create flashcards and drill yourself on any area that you makes you anxious.

Other Helpful Study and Testing Tips

What you study is as important as **how** you study. You can increase your chances of mastering the information by taking some simple, effective steps.

Study Tips

1. You are what you eat. Certain foods aid the learning process by releasing natural memory enhancers called CCKs (cholecystokinin) composed of tryptophan, choline, and phenylalanine. All of these chemicals enhance the neurotransmitters associated with memory and certain foods release memory enhancing chemicals. A light meal or snacks from the following foods fall into this category:

    - Milk
    - Nuts and seeds
    - Rice
    - Oats
    - Eggs
    - Turkey
    - Fish

The better the connections, the more you comprehend!

2. The pen is mightier than the sword. Learn to take great notes. A by-product of our modern culture is that we have grown accustomed to getting our information in short doses. We've subconsciously trained ourselves to assimilate information into neat little packages. Messy notes fragment the flow of information. Your notes can be much clearer with proper formatting. *The Cornell Method* is one such format. This method was popularized in *How to Study in College,* Ninth Edition, by Walter Pauk. You can benefit from the method without purchasing an additional book by simply looking the method up online. On the next page is a sample of how *The Cornell Method* can be adapted for use with this guide.

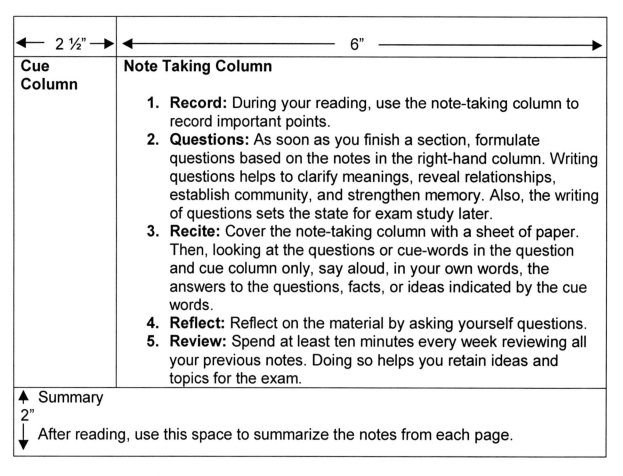

← 2 ½" →	← ————————— 6" ————————— →
Cue Column	**Note Taking Column** 1. **Record:** During your reading, use the note-taking column to record important points. 2. **Questions:** As soon as you finish a section, formulate questions based on the notes in the right-hand column. Writing questions helps to clarify meanings, reveal relationships, establish community, and strengthen memory. Also, the writing of questions sets the state for exam study later. 3. **Recite:** Cover the note-taking column with a sheet of paper. Then, looking at the questions or cue-words in the question and cue column only, say aloud, in your own words, the answers to the questions, facts, or ideas indicated by the cue words. 4. **Reflect:** Reflect on the material by asking yourself questions. 5. **Review:** Spend at least ten minutes every week reviewing all your previous notes. Doing so helps you retain ideas and topics for the exam.

↑ Summary
2"
↓ After reading, use this space to summarize the notes from each page.

*Adapted from *How to Study in College,* Ninth Edition, by Walter Pauk, ©2008 Wadsworth

3. See the forest for the trees. In other words, get the concept before you look at the details. One way to do this is to take notes as you read, paraphrasing or summarizing in your own words. Putting the concept in terms that are comfortable and familiar may increase retention.

4. Question authority. Ask why, why, why. Pull apart written material paragraph by paragraph and don't forget the captions under the illustrations. For example, if a heading reads *Stream Erosion* put it in the form of a question (why do streams erode? Or what is stream erosion?) Then find the answer within the material. If you train your mind to think in this manner you will learn more and prepare yourself for answering test questions.

5. Play mind games. Using your brain for reading or puzzles keeps it flexible. Even with a limited amount of time your brain can take in data (much like a computer) and store it for later use. In ten minutes you can: read two paragraphs (at least), quiz yourself with flash cards, or review notes. Even if you don't fully understand something on the first pass, your mind stores it for recall, which is why frequent reading or review increases chances of retention and comprehension.

6. Place yourself in exile and set the mood. Set aside a particular place and time to study that best suits your personal needs and biorhythms. If you're a night person, burn the midnight oil. If you're a morning person set yourself up with some coffee and get to it. Make your study time and place as free from distraction as possible and surround yourself with what you need, be it silence or music. Studies have shown that music can aid in concentration, absorption, and retrieval of information. Not all music, though. Classical music is said to work best.

7. Get pointed in the right direction. Use arrows to point to important passages or pieces of information. It's easier to read than a page full of yellow highlights. Highlighting can be used sparingly, but add an arrow to the margin to call attention to it.

8. Check your budget. You should at least review all the content material before your test, but allocate the most amount of time to the areas that need the most refreshing. It sounds obvious, but it's easy to forget. You can use the study rubric above to balance your study budget.

> The proctor will write the start time where it can be seen and then, later, provide the time remaining, typically 15 minutes before the end of the test.

And Another Thing

Question Types

You're probably thinking, enough already, I want to study! Indulge us a little longer while we explain that there is actually more than one type of multiple-choice question. You can thank us later after you realize how well prepared you are for your exam.

1. **Complete the Statement.** The name says it all. In this question type you'll be asked to choose the correct completion of a given statement. For example: The Dolch Basic Sight Words consist of a relatively short list of words that children should be able to:

   a. Sound out
   b. Know the meaning of
   c. Recognize on sight
   d. Use in a sentence

   The correct answer is A. In order to check your answer, test out the statement by adding the choices to the end of it.

2. **Which of the Following.** One way to test your answer choice for this type of question is to replace the phrase "which of the following" with your selection. Use this example: Which of the following words is one of the twelve most frequently used in children's reading texts:

   a. There
   b. This
   c. The
   d. An

   Don't look! Test your answer. _____ is one of the twelve most frequently used in children's reading texts. Did you guess C? Then you guessed correctly.

3. **Roman Numeral Choices.** This question type is used when there is more than one possible correct answer. For example: Which of the following two arguments accurately supports the use of cooperative learning as an effective method of instruction?

    I.   Cooperative learning groups facilitate healthy competition between individuals in the group.
    II.   Cooperative learning groups allow academic achievers to carry or cover for academic underachievers.
    III.   Cooperative learning groups make each student in the group accountable for the success of the group.
    IV.   Cooperative learning groups make it possible for students to reward other group members for achieving.

        A. I and II
        B. II and III
        C. I and III
        D. III and IV

Notice that the question states there are **two** possible answers. It's best to read all the possibilities first before looking at the answer choices. In this case, the correct answer is D.

4. **Negative Questions.** This type of question contains words such as "not," "least," and "except." Each correct answer will be the statement that does **not** fit the situation described in the question. Such as: Multicultural education is **not**

    a. An idea or concept
    b. A "tack-on" to the school curriculum
    c. An educational reform movement
    d. A process

Think to yourself that the statement could be anything but the correct answer. This question form is more open to interpretation than other types, so read carefully and don't forget that you're answering a negative statement.

5. **Questions That Include Graphs, Tables, or Reading Passages.** As ever, read the question carefully. It likely asks for a very specific answer and not broad interpretation of the visual. Here is a simple (though not statistically accurate) example of a graph question: In the following graph in how many years did more men take the PRAXIS II exam than women?

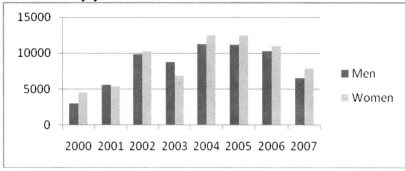

   a. None
   b. One
   c. Two
   d. Three

It may help you to simply circle the two years that answer the question. Make sure you've read the question thoroughly and once you've made your determination, double check your work. The correct answer is C.

Testing Tips

1. Get smart, play dumb. Sometimes a question is just a question. No one is out to trick you, so don't assume that the test writer is looking for something other than what was asked. Stick to the question as written and don't overanalyze.

2. Do a double take. Read test questions and answer choices at least twice because it's easy to miss something, to transpose a word or some letters. If you have no idea what the correct answer is, skip it and come back later if there's time. If you're still clueless, it's okay to guess. Remember, you're scored on the number of questions you answer correctly and you're not penalized for wrong answers. The worst case scenario is that you miss a point from a good guess.

3. Turn it on its ear. The syntax of a question can often provide a clue, so make things interesting and turn the question into a statement to see if it changes the meaning or relates better (or worse) to the answer choices.

4. Get out your magnifying glass. Look for hidden clues in the questions because it's difficult to write a multiple-choice question without giving away part of the answer in the options presented. In most questions you can readily eliminate one or two potential answers, increasing your chances of answering correctly to 50/50, which will help out if you've skipped a question and gone back to it (see tip #2).

5. Call it intuition. Often your first instinct is correct. If you've been studying the content you've likely absorbed something and have subconsciously retained the knowledge. On questions you're not sure about trust your instincts because a first impression is usually correct.

6. Graffiti. Sometimes it's a good idea to mark your answers directly on the test booklet and go back to fill in the optical scan sheet later. You don't get extra points for perfectly blackened ovals. If you choose to manage your test this way, be sure not to mismark your answers when you transcribe to the scan sheet.

7. Become a clock-watcher. You have a set amount of time to answer the questions. Don't get bogged down laboring over a question you're not sure about when there are ten others you could answer more readily. If you choose to follow the advice of tip #6, be sure you leave time near the end to go back and fill in the scan sheet.

Ready? Ready.

Do the Drill

No matter how prepared you feel it's sometimes a good idea to apply Murphy's Law. So the following tips might seem silly, mundane, or obvious, but we're including them anyway.

1. Remember, you are what you eat, so bring a snack. Choose from the list of energizing foods that appear earlier in the introduction.
2. You're not too sexy for your test. Wear comfortable clothes. You'll be distracted if your belt is too tight, or if you're too cold or too hot.
3. Lie to yourself. Even if you think you're a prompt person, pretend you're not and leave plenty of time to get to the testing center. Map it out ahead of time and do a dry run if you have to. There's no need to add road rage to your list of anxieties.
4. Bring **sharp, number 2 pencils.** It may seem impossible to forget this need from your school days, but you might. And make sure the erasers are intact, too.
5. No ticket, no test. Bring your admission ticket as well as **two** forms of identification, including one with a picture and signature. You will not be admitted to the test without these things.
6. You can't take it with you. Leave any study aids, dictionaries, notebooks, computers and the like at home. Certain tests **do** allow a scientific or four-function calculator, so check ahead of time if your test does.
7. Prepare for the desert. Any time spent on a bathroom break **cannot** be made up later, so use your judgment on the amount you eat or drink.
8. Quiet, Please! Keeping your own time is a good idea, but not with a timepiece that has a loud ticker. If you use a watch, take it off and place it nearby but not so that it distracts you. And **silence your cell phone.**

To the best of our ability, the content you need to know is represented in this book and in the accompanying online resources. The rest is up to you. You can use the study and testing tips or you can follow your own methods. Either way, you can be confident that there aren't any missing pieces of information and there shouldn't be any surprises in the content on the test.

Good luck!

TABLE OF CONTENTS

SUBAREA I.   **FOUNDATIONS OF ESOL INSTRUCTION**

COMPETENCY 1.0   **UNDERSTAND BASIC LINGUISTIC CONCEPTS AND THEIR APPLICATION TO ESOL INSTRUCTION**

Skill 1.1   Applying knowledge of phonetics and phonology (e.g., distinguishing among classes of sound).. 1

Skill 1.2   Applying knowledge of English morphology and lexicon to analyze a word's structure, function, and meaning 3

Skill 1.3   Identifying syntactic features (e.g., a verb phrase) in sentence context 5

Skill 1.4   Identifying discourse features (e.g., cohesion) in a textual context. 7

Skill 1.5   Applying knowledge of linguistic concepts in interlanguage analysis 9

Skill 1.6   Applying knowledge of the structure of the English language 11

COMPETENCY 2.0   **UNDERSTAND BASIC SOCIOLINGUISTIC CONCEPTS RELATED TO ESOL INSTRUCTION 13**

Skill 2.1   Demonstrating knowledge of sociolinguistic concepts (e.g., dialect diversity in English, intercultural differences in communication styles, codeswitching)... 13

Skill 2.2   Demonstrating knowledge of academic discourses.......................... 15

Skill 2.3   Demonstrating knowledge of language variation............................. 16

Skill 2.4   Demonstrating knowledge of the appropriate roles of written and spoken Standard English.. 17

COMPETENCY 3.0   **UNDERSTAND THE PROCESS OF LANGUAGE ACQUISITION 19**

Skill 3.1   Analyzing major theories of first- and second- language acquisition 19

Skill 3.2   Demonstrating knowledge of stages, and sequences in second-language acquisition in terms of the learners' individual characteristics...21

Skill 3.3   Demonstrating knowledge of the learning processes (e.g., metacognitive and cognitive strategies) that are involved in internalizing language rules for second- language acquisition 22

Skill 3.4   Applying knowledge of the role of the first language in second-language acquisition and learning (e.g., language transfer, interlanguage development) 24

COMPETENCY 4.0   UNDERSTAND INSTRUCTIONAL APPROACHES, METHODS, AND TECHNIQUES IN SECOND-LANGUAGE ACQUISITION AND LEARNING............ 26

Skill 4.1   Analyzing the theoretical bases of historical and current instructional approaches (e.g. communicative language teaching, functional- notional approach, content- based language instruction, theme- based language instruction) 26

Skill 4.2   Applying strategies for integrating assessment with second-language instruction 29

Skill 4.3   Selecting classroom activities to accommodate the diverse needs of learners and instructional methods...30

Skill 4.4   Choosing appropriate instructional practices to achieve curricular objectives 32

Skill 4.5   Demonstrating knowledge of classroom organization strategies to create opportunities for meaningful communication 35

COMPETENCY 5.0   UNDERSTAND FACTORS THAT MAY INFLUENCE ENGLISH LANGUAGE LEARNERS' DEVELOPMENT OF ENGLISH..................................37

Skill 5.1   Analyzing cultural and environmental factors that may affect students' English language development (e.g., age, motivation).......
....37

Skill 5.2   Analyzing social and psychological factors that may affect students' English language development (e.g., personality, cultural transition)
....39

Skill 5.3   Demonstrating knowledge of nonlinguistic and sociocultural aspects of English that are challenging for English language learners (e.g., idioms, nonverbal elements, turn- taking features) 40

Skill 5.4   Demonstrating knowledge of the ways in which educational background may affect literacy development 42

COMPETENCY 6.0   UNDERSTAND METHODS AND TECHNIQUES FOR ASSESSING STUDENTS' PROGRESS IN DEVELOPING ENGLISH COMMUNICATION SKILLS 43

Skill 6.1   Demonstrating knowledge of different types of assessments (e.g., norm and criterion- referenced, standardized, informal) and important concepts used in evaluating the usefulness and appropriateness of an assessment (e.g., reliability, validity, practicality) 43

Skill 6.2   Analyzing formal and informal methods of assessing specific dimensions of language proficiency..44

Skill 6.3   Demonstrating knowledge of informal assessment strategies and approaches (e.g., observational checklists)....................................46

Skill 6.4   Demonstrating an understanding of sources and causes of potential bias in assessment...48

SUBAREA II.   DEVELOPING ENGLISH LANGUAGE PROFICIENCY ACROSS THE CURRICULUM

COMPETENCY 7.0   UNDERSTAND METHODS AND TECHNIQUES FOR DEVELOPING AND ASSESSING THE LISTENING PROFICIENCY OF ENGLISH LANGUAGE LEARNERS 50

Skill 7.1   Analyzing the role of prior knowledge in aural comprehension..........
....50

Skill 7.2   Demonstrating knowledge of listening skills required in different situations (e.g., listening for gist vs. listening for details, listening to a lecture vs. listening to the context of a conversation) 51

Skill 7.3   Selecting appropriate classroom listening activities to achieve given instructional purposes...52

Skill 7.4   Selecting appropriate classroom listening activities that build o and expand students' real- life situations and experiences 53

Skill 7.5 54

COMPETENCY 8.0   UNDERSTAND METHODS AND TECHNIQUES FOR DEVELOPING AND ASSESSING THE SPEAKING SKILLS OF ENGLISH LANGUAGE LEARNERS ....
....55

Skill 8.1   Accommodating and identifying the instructional needs of students at various levels of oral proficiency...55

Skill 8.2   Selecting appropriate classroom speaking activities (e.g., paired and small- group conversations, choral speaking, creative drama, role playing) to meet varied instructional purposes 57

Skill 8.3   Selecting appropriate classroom strategies to extend students' communicative competence and social interaction skills..................58

Skill 8.4   Applying knowledge of the role of oral language in literacy development...59

Skill 8.5   Selecting or creating appropriate assessments for given testing purposes and situations..60

COMPETENCY 9.0   UNDERSTAND METHODS AND TECHNIQUES FOR DEVELOPING AND ASSESSING THE READING PROFICIENCY OF ENGLISH LANGUAGE LEARNERS, FOR THE DUAL PURPOSES OF LEARNING TO READ AND READING TO LEARN....
....62

Skill 9.1   Demonstrating knowledge of principles of effective reading instruction..62

Skill 9.2   Demonstrating knowledge of the transferability of first- language literacy skills into English..64

Skill 9.3   Identifying strategies that help English language learners utilize their spoken English to develop their reading proficiency in English (e.g., language experience approach)...65

Skill 9.4   Demonstrating knowledge of the interrelationship between decoding and comprehension in English...65

Skill 9.5   Applying knowledge of schema theory in reading instruction 66

Skill 9.6   Applying knowledge of various literary genres and purposes for reading 66

Skill 9.7   Selecting and adapting appropriate classroom activities for given instructional purposes and for English language learners at different literacy levels and English language proficiency levels 68

Skill 9.8   Selecting or creating appropriate assessments for given testing purposes and situations..71

COMPETENCY 10.0   **UNDERSTAND METHODS AND TECHNIQUES FOR DEVELOPING AND ASSESSING THE WRITING SKILLS OF ENGLISH LANGUAGE LEARNERS ....** **74**

Skill 10.1   Analyzing the role of other communicative modes (e.g. speaking, reading) in developing the writing skills of English language learners 74

Skill 10.2   Applying knowledge of the writing process in designing activities to develop students' writing proficiency 75

Skill 10.3   Identifying strategies for developing students' organization in writing and their ability to write in different academic genres (e.g., narration, analysis) 78

Skill 10.4   Selecting purposeful writing activities that are appropriate to a range of ages and proficiency levels (e.g., friendly letters, book reports, research papers) 79

Skill 10.5   Applying instructional strategies that address conventions of English grammar, usage, and mechanics.......................................81

Skill 10.6   Selecting or creating appropriate assessments for given testing purposes and situations..83

COMPETENCY 11.0   **UNDERSTAND THE SELECTION, ADAPTATION, AND USE OF MATERIALS FOR VARIOUS INSTRUCTIONAL PURPOSES IN THE ESOL CLASSROOM**...**85**

Skill 11.1   Defining appropriate criteria for evaluating instructional materials 85

Skill 11.2   Selecting appropriate materials for given instructional purposes (e.g., making content accessible) 86

Skill 11.3   Demonstrating knowledge of the uses of content- area texts, children's and adolescent literature, and multicultural literature in the ESOL classroom 87

Skill 11.4   Creating and adapting materials to meet the needs, interests, and proficiency levels of students 89

Skill 11.5   Recognizing ways to integrate technologies in the classroom for given instructional purposes 90

COMPETENCY 12.0   UNDERSTAND APPROACHES TO FACILITATING CONTENT- AREA LEARNING FOR ENGLISH LANGUAGE LEARNERS 93

Skill 12.1   Demonstrating knowledge of techniques for using students' linguistic and cultural diversity to enhance content- area learning 93

Skill 12.2   Identifying linguistic characteristics and applying methods for developing students' cognitive- academic language proficiency in content areas 94

Skill 12.3   Demonstrate the ability to devise and implement thematic units that integrate content and language objectives and help English language learners to acquire content- area knowledge and skills 96

Skill 12.4   Utilizing strategies for selecting and adapting content- area curricula to meet the cognitive and linguistic needs of English language learners 98

Skill 12.5   Applying knowledge of instructional strategies that help students build on their prior knowledge and experience 99

Skill 12.6   Analyzing the benefits of collaboration between the ESOL teacher and content- area teachers 101

SUBAREA III.   THE ESOL PROGRAM

COMPETENCY 13   UNDERSTAND HISTORICAL, LEGAL AND ADMINISTRATIVE ASPECTS OF PROGRAMS SERVING ENGLISH LANGUAGE LEARNERS 102

Skill 13.1   Demonstrating knowledge of historical and current issues related to ESOL instruction..102

Skill 13.2   Applying the provisions of federal and state laws and regulations governing the delivery of ESOL instruction.......................103

Skill 13.3   Analyzing knowledge of the roles and responsibilities of teachers, parents and others in the education of English language learners.... 104

Skill 13.4   Demonstrating understanding of the relationship between the ESOL program and other school programs................................105

COMPETENCY 14   UNDERSTAND APPROACHES TO INSTRUCTION THAT ARE APPROPRIATE TO THE DIVERSITY OF THE ENGLISH LANGUAGE LEARNER POPULATION AND THAT MEET VARIOUS STUDENT NEEDS.......................107

Skill 14.1   Recognizing cross- cultural and linguistic differences in communication styles (e.g., rhetorical styles, conversational styles). 107

Skill 14.2   Demonstrating knowledge of ways to acknowledge and affirm various types of diversity in the ESOL classroom, the school, and the community 107

Skill 14.3   Applying knowledge of assessments to determine whether students' needs are based on language differences and/or language disorders..109

Skill 14.4   Making appropriate instructional adaptations for English language learners with special educational needs (e.g., learning disabilities, giftedness) and for learners whose previous formal academic instruction has been severely interrupted................................111

Skill 14.5   Selecting and applying instructional strategies appropriate to students' varied learning styles 112

COMPETENCY 15   UNDERSTAND THE PLANNING AND MANAGEMENT OF ESOL INSTRUCTION IN A VARIETY OF SETTINGS..117

Skill 15.1   Demonstrating an understanding of different settings/models of ESOL instruction (e.g., sheltered instruction, integrated programs) and management strategies appropriate to each 117

Skill 15.2   Selecting appropriate ways to organize instruction for students at different ages, stages of cognitive development, and proficiency levels 118

Skill 15.3   Selecting appropriate ways of grouping students for instructional purposes..120

COMPETENCY 16   UNDERSTAND THE METHODS OF RELATING ESOL INSTRUCTION TO STUDENTS' LIVES OUTSIDE THE CLASSROOM......................................123

Skill 16.1   Demonstrating knowledge of ways to encourage active involvement of families of English language learners in the instructional program 123

Skill 16.2   Applying methods of facilitating communication between the school and families of English language learners 123

Skill 16.3   Analyzing the potential uses of home and community resources in the ESOL program...123

Sample Test 124

Answer Key 150

Rigor Table 151

Rationales 152

COMPETENCY 1.0   UNDERSTAND BASIC LINGUISTIC CONCEPTS AND THEIR APPLICATION TO ESOL INSTRUCTION

Skill 1.1   Applying knowledge of phonetics and phonology (e.g. distinguishing between classes of sound)

The definition of phonology can be summarized as "the way in which speech sounds form patterns" (Díaz-Rico & Weed, 1995). Phonology is a subset of the linguistics field, which studies the organization and systems of sound within a particular language. Phonology is based on the theory that every native speaker unconsciously retains the sound structure of that language and is more concerned with the sounds than with the physical process of creating those sounds.

When babies babble or make what we call "baby talk," they are actually experimenting with all of the sounds represented in all languages. As they learn a specific language, they become more proficient in the sounds of that language and forget how to make sounds that they don't need or use.

Phonemes, pitch, and stress are all components of phonology. Because each affects the meaning of communications, they are variables that ELLs must recognize and learn. Phonology analyzes the sound structure of the given language by:

- Determining which phonetic sounds have the most significance
- Explaining how these sounds influence a native speaker of the language

For example, the Russian alphabet has a consonant, which, when pronounced, sounds like the word "rouge" in French. English speakers typically have difficulty pronouncing this sound pattern, because inherently they know this is not a typical English sound-- even though it occasionally is encountered (Díaz-Rico & Weed, 1995).

Mastering a sound that does not occur in the learner's first language requires ongoing repetition, both of hearing the sound and attempting to say it. The older the learner, the more difficult this becomes, especially if the learner has only spoken one language before reaching puberty. Correct pronunciation may literally require years of practice because initially the learner may not hear the sound correctly. Expecting an ELL to master a foreign pronunciation quickly leads to frustration for the teacher and the learner. With enough focused repetition, however, the learner may eventually hear the difference and then be able to imitate it. Inadequate listening and speaking practice will result in a persistent heavy accent.

Phonemes are the smallest unit of sound that affects meaning, i.e. distinguish two words. In English, there are approximately 44 speech sounds yet only 26 letters, so the sounds, when combined, become words. For this reason, English is not considered a phonetic language where there is a one-to-one correspondence between letters and sounds. For example, consider the two words, "pin" and "bin." The only difference is the first consonant of the words, the "p" in "pin" and "b" in "bin." This makes the sounds "p" and "b" phonemes in English, because the difference in sound creates a difference in meaning.

Focusing on phonemes to provide pronunciation practice allows students to have fun while they learn to recognize and say sounds. Pairs or groups of words that have a set pattern make learning easier. For example, students can practice saying or thinking of words that rhyme but begin with a different phoneme, such as tan, man, fan, and ran. Other groups of words might start with the same phoneme followed by various vowel sounds, such as ten, ton, tan, and tin. This kind of alliteration can be expanded into tongue twisters that students find challenging and fun.

Vowels and consonants should be introduced in a deliberate order to allow combinations that form real words, though "made-up" words that have no real meaning in English should also be encouraged when introducing new sounds.

Pitch in communication determines the context or meaning of words or series of words. A string of words can communicate more than one meaning; for example, when posed as a question or statement. For example, the phrase "I can't go" acts as a statement, if the pitch or intonation falls. However, the same phrase becomes the question "I can't go?" if the pitch or intonation rises for the word "go."

Stress can occur at a "word" or "sentence" level. At the "word" level, different stresses on the syllable can actually modify the word's meaning. Consider the word "conflict." To pronounce it as a noun, one would stress the first syllable, as in "CONflict." However, to use it as a verb, the second syllable would be stressed, as in "conFLICT."

Different dialects sometimes pronounce the same word differently, even though both pronunciations have the same meaning. For example, in some parts of the United States the word "insurance" is pronounced by stressing the second syllable, while in other parts of the country the first syllable is stressed.

At the "sentence" level, stress can also be used to vary the meaning. For example, consider the following questions and how the meaning changes, according to the stressed words:

> **He** did that? (Emphasis is on the person)
> He **did** that? (Emphasis is on the action)
> He did **that**? (Emphasis is on object of the action)

This type of meaning differentiation is difficult for most ELL students to grasp and requires innovative teaching, such as acting out the three different meanings. However, since pitch and stress can change the meaning of a sentence completely, students must learn to recognize these differences. Not recognizing sarcasm or anger can cause students considerable problems in their academic and everyday endeavors.

Unlike languages such as Spanish or French, English has multiple pronunciations of vowels and consonants, which contributes to making it a difficult language to learn. While phonetic rules are critical to learning to read and write, in spite of there being numerous exceptions, they do little to assist listening and speaking skills.

Skill 1.2   Applying knowledge of English morphology and lexicon to analyze a word's structure, function, and meaning.

Morphology refers to the process of how the words of a language are formed to create meaningful messages. ESOL teachers need to be aware of the principles of morphology in English to provide meaningful activities that will help in the process of language acquisition.

Morphemic analysis requires breaking a word down into its component parts to determine its meaning. It shows the relationship between the root or base word and the prefix and/or suffix to determine the word's meaning.

A morpheme is the smallest unit of language system which has meaning. These units are more commonly known as: the root word, the prefix and the suffix, and they cannot be broken down into any smaller units.

- **The root word or base word** is the key to understanding a word, because this is where the actual meaning is determined.
- **A prefix** acts as a syllable, which appears in front of the root or base word and can alter the meaning of the root or base word.
- **A suffix** is a letter or letters, which are added to the end of the word and can alter the original tense or meaning of the root or base word.

The following is an example of how morphemic analysis can be applied to a word:

- Choose a root or base word, such as "kind."
- Create as many new words as possible, by changing the prefix and suffix.
- New words, would include unkind, kindness, and kindly.

Learning common roots, prefixes, and suffixes greatly helps ELLs to decode unfamiliar words. This can make a big difference in how well a student understands written language. Students who can decode unfamiliar words become less frustrated when reading in English and, as a result, are likely to read more. They have greater comprehension and their language skills improve more quickly. Having the tools to decode unfamiliar words enables ELLs to perform better on standardized tests because they are more likely to understand the questions and answer choices.

Guessing at the meaning of words should be encouraged. To ooften students become dependent on translation dictionaries, which cause the students not to develop morphemic analysis skills. Practice should include identifying roots, prefixes, and suffixes, as well as using morphemic knowledge to form new words.

ESOL learners need to understand the structure of words in English, and how words may be created and altered. Some underlying principles of the morphology of English are:

1. Morphemes may be free and able to stand by themselves (e.g., chair, bag) or they may be bound or derivational, needing to be used with other morphemes to create meaning (e.g., read-able, en-able).
2. Knowledge of the meanings of derivational morphemes such as prefixes and suffixes enables students to decode word meanings and create words in the language through word analysis, e.g., un-happy means not happy.
3. Some morphemes in English provide grammatical rather than semantic information for words and sentences (e.g., of, the, and).
4. Words can be combined in English to create new compound words (e.g., key + chain = keychain).

ESOL teachers also need to be aware that principles of morphology from the native language may be transferred to either promote or interfere with the second language learning process.

Semantics encompasses the meaning of individual words, as well as combinations of words. Native speakers have used their language to function in their daily lives at all levels. Through experience they know the effects of intonation, connotation, and synonyms. This is not true of foreign speakers. In an ESOL class, we are trying to teach what the native speaker already knows as quickly as possible. The objectives of beginning ESOL lesson plans should deliberately build a foundation that will enable students to meet more advanced objectives.

Teaching within a specific context helps students to understand the meaning of words and sentences. When students can remember the context in which they learn words and recall how the words were used, they retain that knowledge and can compare it when different applications of the same words are introduced.

Using words in a variety of contexts helps students reach a deeper understanding of the word. They can then guess at new meanings that are introduced in different contexts. For example, the word "conduct" can be taught in the context of conducting a meeting or an investigation. Later the word "conductor" can be used in various contexts that demonstrate some similarity but have distinctly different uses of the word, such as a conductor of electricity; the conductor of a train; the conductor of an orchestra; and so forth.

Skill 1.3   Identifying syntactic features (e.g., a verb phrase) in sentence context.

A sentence is a group of words that has a subject and predicate, and expresses a complete idea. A subject tells us what or whom the sentence is about and the predicate makes a statement about what the subject is or does. Subjects and predicates can be modified and combined in different ways to make simple, compound or complex sentences. (In all the following examples, subjects are underlined and predicates italicized.)

Example: The snow *falls quietly.*

Subject: The subject, or the topic of a sentence, consists of a noun or a pronoun and all the words that modify it. "The snow" is the subject in the above example. The simple subject is the main part of the subject. "Snow" is the simple subject.

Predicate: The predicate makes a statement or a comment about the subject and it consists of a verb and all the words that modify it; "falls quietly" is the predicate in the above example. The simple predicate is the main part of the predicate and is always the verb; "falls" is the simple predicate.

Compound subject: When the subject consists of two or more pronouns, e.g. Books and magazines *filled the room.*

Compound predicate: A predicate that contains more than one verb pertaining to the subject, e.g., The boys *walked and talked.*

Sentences in English are of three types:

Simple Sentence: A simple sentence, or independent clause, is a complete thought consisting of a subject and a predicate:
The bus *was late.*

Compound Sentence: A compound sentence consists of two independent clauses joined together by a coordinator (and, or, nor, but, for, yet, so):
Tom *walked to the bus station* **and** he *took the bus.*

Complex Sentence: A complex sentence is a sentence consisting of a dependent clause (a group words with a subject and predicate that are not a complete thought) and an independent clause joined together using a subordinator (although, after, when, because, since, while):
After I write the report, I will submit it to my teacher.

Sentences serve different purposes. They can make a statement (declarative); ask a question (interrogative); give a command (imperative); or express a sense of urgency (exclamatory). Understanding the different purposes for sentences can help ELLs understand the relationship between what they write and the ideas they want to express.

ELLs often over-generalize that sentence fragments are short and complete sentences are long. When they truly understand what constitutes a sentence, they will realize that length has nothing to do with whether a sentence is complete or not. For example:

> "He ran." is a complete sentence.
> "After the very funny story began" is a fragment

To make these distinctions, learners must know the parts of speech and understand the difference between independent clauses, dependent clauses, and phrases.

Phrase: a group of words that does not have a subject and a predicate and cannot stand alone. The most common types of phrases are prepositional (in the room); participial (walking down the street); and infinitive (to run).

Parts of speech: the eight classifications for words. Each part of speech has a specific role in sentences. This can be quite difficult for ELLs because the same word can have a different role in different sentences, and a different meaning entirely. Identifying the subject and predicate of the sentence helps to distinguish what role a particular word plays in a sentence. Since English is an S-V-O language, the placement of a word in a sentence relative to the subject or verb indicates what part of speech it is.

- That TV **show** was boring.
- I will **show** you my new dress.
- The band plays **show** tunes at half-time.

In these examples, the word **show** is first a noun, then a verb, and finally an adjective.

The parts of speech include:

Noun: a person, place, thing or idea. Common nouns are non-specific, while proper nouns name a particular person, place, thing, or idea, and are capitalized.

Verb: an action or state of being.

Pronoun: a word that takes the place of a noun.
Personal pronouns can be

- first, second, or third person (I, you, he, she it);
- singular or plural (I/we, you/you, he, she, it/they); and
- subjective or objective (I/me, you/you, he/him, she/her, it/it, we/us, they/them).

Possessive pronouns show ownership (my, mine, your, yours, his, her, hers, its, our, ours, your, yours, their, and theirs).

Indefinite pronouns refer to persons, places, things or ideas in general, such as any, each, both, most, something.

Adjective: a word that modifies a noun or pronoun. They answer the questions, *What kind? How many?* and *Which?*

Adverb: a word that modifies a verb, and adjective, or another adverb. They answer the questions, *How? When? Where? How often?* and *To what extent?*

Prepositions: occur in a phrase with a noun or pronoun and show the relationship between a noun or pronoun and another word in a sentence. They describe, or show location, direction, or time. Prepositional phrases can have as few as two words, but can include any number or adjectives.
Interjection: a word that shows surprise or strong feeling. It can stand alone (Help!) or be used within a sentence (Oh no, I forgot my wallet!)

Constructing sentences involves combining words in grammatically correct ways to communicate the desired thought. Avoiding fragments and run-ons requires continual sentence analysis. The test of a complete sentence is: Does it contain a subject and predicate and express a complete idea? Practice identifying independent clauses, dependent clauses, and phrases will help ELLs to write complete sentences.

Sill 1.4   Identifying discourse features (e.g., cohesion) in a textual context

The term discourse refers to linguistic units composed of several sentences and is derived from the concept of "discursive formation" or communication that involves specialized knowledge of various kinds. Conversations, arguments, or speeches are types of discourses. Discourse shapes the way language is transmitted, and also how we organize our thoughts.

The structure of discourse varies among languages and traditions. For example, Japanese writing does not present the main idea at the beginning of an essay; rather, writing builds up to the main idea, which is presented or implied at the end of the essay. This is completely different than English writing, which typically presents the main idea or thesis at the beginning of an essay and repeats it at the end.

In addition to language and structure, topic or focus affects discourse. The discourse in various disciplines approach topics differently, such as feminist studies, cultural studies, and literary theory. Discourse plays a role in all spoken and written language, and affects our thinking.

Written discourse ranges from the most basic grouping of sentences to the most complicated essays and stories. Regardless of the level, English writing demands certain structure patterns. A typical paragraph begins with a topic sentence, which states directly or indirectly the focus of the paragraph; adds supporting ideas and details; and ends with a concluding sentence that relates to the focus and either states the final thought on that topic or provides a transition to the next paragraph when there are more than one. As with spoken discourse, organization, tone, and word choice are critical to transferring thoughts successfully and maintaining interest.

As skills increase, paragraphs are combined into stories or essays. Each type of writing has specific components and structures. Story writing requires setting, plot, and character. Initially, following a chronological order is probably easiest for ELLs, but as learners become more skillful, other types of order should be practiced, such as adding descriptions in spatial order,

Teachers frequently rely on the proverbial three- or five-paragraph essay to teach essay writing because it provides a rigid structure for organizing and expanding ideas within a single focus. It mirrors the paragraph structure organizationally in that the first, introductory paragraph provides the main idea or focus of the essay; each body paragraph adds and develops a supporting idea and details; and the concluding paragraph provides a summary or other type of conclusion that relates to the main idea or focus stated in the first paragraph. Obviously no one considers such mechanical essays to be the ultimate goal of essay writing. However, especially for ELLs, having a rigid structure teaches the basic organizational concept of English essays. By offering strictly defined limits, the teacher reduces the number of variables to learn about essay writing. Starting with a blank page can be overwhelming to ELLs. Working within this structure enables learners to focus on developing each paragraph, a challenging enough task when one considers the language skills required! As learners become better able to control their writing and sustain a focus, variations can be introduced and topics expanded.

Skill 1.5   Applying knowledge of linguistic concepts in interlanguage analysis.

During the acquisition of a second language, learners develop a linguistic system that is complete in itself and is different from both the learner's first language and the target language. Interlanguage is a temporary and changing grammatical system which approximates that of the language being learned. In the process of L2 acquisition, interlanguage (IL) continuously evolves getting more and more like the target language. Ideally, the second language learner's IL should become equivalent or nearly equivalent to the target language. However, for various reasons, at times IL may cease to grow and does not become like the target language. This is termed as *fossilization* (Selinker, 1972), where the progress in the acquisition of L2 terminates despite repeated efforts.

Interlanguage can be a cause of several different processes. These include (a) borrowing patterns from the mother tongue, (b) extending patterns from the target language, (c) expressing meaning using the words and grammar which are already known (Richards, 1992). Because IL is a development process, teachers can give appropriate feedback for further improvement. Similarly, learners should not be worried about making mistakes as it is a natural process on the continuum of second language acquisition. This gives learners margin for errors and relieves them from constant supervision by the teachers thus leading to pair and group work.
Interlanguage consists of a structural simplification, e.g., omission of all morphological marking, fixed word order, reduced vocabulary, etc. Another example is the acquisition of relative clauses. Some languages like English and Arabic have relative clause while others, like Japanese and Chinese, do not (Ellis, 1997). Therefore, learners whose L1 has relative clause will learn them more easily an will not avoid using them then those that lack this lexical feature in their L1. The linguistic aspect of relative clause affects another way, too. In English, the relative clause

- Can be attached to the end of the main clause, e.g, The ambulance took the woman to the hospital who was struck by lightening.
- Can be embedded in the main clause, e.g., The woman who was struck by lightening was taken to the hospital by the ambulance.

Second language learners typically acquire the first type of relative clause with more ease than the later. Furthermore, studies have also shown that L2 learners tend to acquire first the relative clause with a subject pronoun (for example, *who*) than with an object pronoun (for example, *whom*). This shows certain predictability in the acquisition of certain structures which would help teachers in developing materials for different levels of students at various proficiency levels.

Chomsky put forward his theory of *universal language* which assumes that all languages have a common structural basis and provides parameters which are given particular settings in different languages. Chomsky based this on his research on L1 acquisition by children. He observes that the input that the children are exposed to is insufficient for them to learn the rules of their target language. Therefore, he hypothesized that these children must rely on innate knowledge of language in order to acquire their respective L1. There is a great debate over the accessibility of UG in second language acquisition.

The above controversy also considers whether the access of universal grammars depends on the age of the language learner called the *critical period hypothesis*. This hypothesis states that there is a period during language acquisition when learners are able to achieve native-like proficiency in the target language. Studies show that L2 learners who began learning as adults are unable to achieve native-like ability in either grammar or pronunciation. However, there is a difference in competence level with respect to L1 and L2 learners. This could be due to the difference in social conditions where L1 learners have a lot of opportunity to interact in their first language. Additionally, it could be because L1 and L2 have separate learning mechanisms because most adult L2 learners do not have access to UG. However, many theories have been postulated with respect to universal grammar in second language acquisition. This ranges from complete access, no access, partial access (L2 learning is partly regulated by UG and partly be general learning strategies) to dual access (rely on both learning strategies and UG, but can only be fully successful if they depend on UG.

Another theory with respect linguistic concepts in interlanguage analysis is the study of *nakedness*. This puts forward the theory that some structures are more common in world's languages than others which are referred to as unmarked whereas marked structures are those that are not common. One hypothesis that emerged from this theory is that the less marked structures are acquired earlier than more marked structures. However, other studies have found out that L2 learners are more likely to acquire a marked structure frequent in input than an unmarked structure that is not used frequently. Furthermore, research has pointed out the role oft L1 transfer in this area. It had been suggested that learners might be able to transfer unmarked structures from their L1 than unmarked structures.

Another set of theories is based on Stephen Krashen's research in L2 acquisition. Most people understand his theories based on five principles:

1. <u>The acquisition-learning hypothesis</u>: There is a difference between learning a language and acquiring it. Children "acquire" a first language easily—it's natural. But adults often have to "learn" a language through coursework, studying, and memorizing. One can acquire a second language, but often it requires more deliberate and natural interaction within that language.
2. <u>The monitor hypothesis</u>: The learned language "monitors" the acquired language. In other words, this is when a person's "grammar check" kicks in and keeps awkward, incorrect language out of a person's L2 communication.

3. <u>The natural order hypothesis</u>: This theory suggests that learning grammatical structures is predictable and follows a "natural order."
4. <u>The input hypothesis</u>: Some people call this "comprehensible input." This means that a language learner will learn best when the instruction or conversation is just above the learner's ability. That way, the learner has the foundation to understand most of the language, but still will have to figure out, often in context, what that extra more difficult element means.
5. <u>The affective filter hypothesis</u>: This theory suggests that people will learn a second language when they are relaxed, have high levels of motivation, and have a decent level of self-confidence.

The above discussion of the L2 learners' interlanguage shows the importance of analyzing the students native language as well as an understanding the linguistic concepts of the target language in order to understand the different stages on L2 development within a classroom. It is important for the teachers to try to introduce new materials based on this analysis and provide learners with appropriate learning strategies that would help them achieve native-like proficiency in the target language.

Skill 1.6   Applying knowledge of the structure of the English language.

Syntax involves the order in which words are arranged to create meaning. Different languages use different patterns for sentence structure. Syntax also refers to the rules for creating correct sentence patterns. English, like many other languages, is a subject-verb-object language, which means that in most sentences the subject precedes the verb, and the object follows the verb. ELLs whose native language follows a subject-verb-object pattern will find it easier to master English syntax.

The process of second language acquisition includes forming generalizations about the new language and internalizing the rules that are observed. During the silent period, before learners are willing to attempt verbal communication, they are engaged in the process of building a set of syntactic rules for creating grammatically correct sentences in the second language. We don't yet fully understand the nature of this process, but we do know that learners must go through this process of observing, drawing conclusions about language constructs, and testing the validity of their conclusions. This is why learners benefit more from intense language immersion than from corrections.

Language acquisition is a gradual, hierarchical, and cumulative process. This means that learners must go through and master each stage in sequence, much as Piaget theorized for learning in general. In terms of syntax, this means learners must acquire specific grammatical structures, first recognizing the difference between subject and predicate; putting subject before predicate; and learning more complex variations, such as questions, negatives, and relative clauses.

While learners much pass through each stage and accumulate the language skills learned in each progressive stage, learners use different approaches to mastering these skills. Some learners use more cognitive processing procedures, which means their learning takes place more through thought processes, while other learners tend to use psycholinguistic procedures, which employs processing learning more through speech. Regardless of how learners process information, they must all proceed through the same stages, from least to most complicate.

Experts disagree on the exact definition of the phases, but a set of six general stages would include:

Stage of Development	Examples
1. Single words	I; throw; ball
2. SVO structure	I throw the ball.
3. Wh- fronting	Where you are?
Do fronting	Do you like me?
Adverb fronting	Today I go to school.
Negative + verb	She is not nice.
4. Y/N inversion	Do you know him? Yes, I know him.
Copula (linking v) inversion	Is he at school?
Particle shift	Take your hat off.
5. Do 2nd	Why did she leave?
Aux 2nd	Where has he gone?
Neg do 2nd	She does not live here.
6. Cancel inversion	I asked what she was doing.

Each progressive step requires the learner to use knowledge from the previous step, as well as new knowledge of the language. As ELLs progress to more advanced stages of syntax, they may react differently depending on their ability to acquire the new knowledge that is required for mastery. A learner who successfully integrates the new knowledge is a "standardizer"; he/she makes generalizations, eliminates erroneous conclusions, and increasingly uses syntactical rules correctly. However, for some learners, the next step may be more difficult than the learner can manage. These learners become "simplifiers"; they revert to syntactical rules learned at easier stages and fail to integrate the new knowledge. When patterns of errors reflect lower level stages, the teacher must re-teach the new syntactical stage. If simplifiers are allowed to repeatedly use incorrect syntax, they risk having their language become fossilized, which makes learning correct syntax that much more difficult.

COMPETENCY 2   UNDERSTAND BASIC SOCIOLINGUISTIC CONCEPTS RELATED TO ESOL INSTRUCTION.

Skill 2.1   Demonstrating knowledge of sociolinguistic concepts (e.g., dialect diversity in English, intercultural differences in communication styles, code switching)

American English usage is influenced by the social and regional situation of its users. Linguists have found that speakers adapt their pronunciation, vocabulary, grammar and sentence structure depending on the social situation. For example, the decision to use – ing or –in at the end of a present participle depends on the formality of the situation. Speakers talking with their friends will often drop the "g" and use of –in to signal that the situation is more informal and relaxed. These variations are also related to factors such as age, gender, education, socioeconomic status, and personality.

We call this type of shift a change in register, how language is used in a particular setting or for a particular purpose. People change their speech register depending on such sociolinguistic variables as:

- Formality of situation
- Attitude towards topic
- Attitude towards listeners
- Relation of speaker to others

Changing speech registers may be completely subconscious for native speakers. For example, if a university professor takes his car in for servicing, the manner and speech he uses to communicate with the mechanic differs significantly from the manner and speech he uses to deliver a lecture. If he were to use a formal tone and academic vocabulary, the mechanic might think the professor was trying to put him down, or he might not understand what the professor was saying. Likewise, when the mechanic explains the mechanical diagnosis, he most likely chooses a simplified vocabulary rather than using completely technical language, or jargon, that the professor wouldn't understand. Using the jargon of any field the listener doesn't know will likely make the listener feel stupid or inferior, and perhaps that the speaker is inconsiderate,

Language registers are also used to deliberately establish a social identity. Hispanics deliberately refer to themselves as La Raza (the race) to imply dignity and pride for what they are and where they come from. Using a Spanish term when speaking English is called code switching. As a result, this term is becoming (or has become) a part of the American vocabulary. Symbolically it represents both the Hispanics' distinction and their integration into American culture.

The growth in popularity of rap demonstrates how and why sociolinguistic changes occur over time. The term "rap" dates back to 16th century Britain and has connections to Celtic music. In the 1960s, Black Americans adopted the term to describe the rhythmic style of speaking they used to distinguish themselves from White Americans.

Their need for distinction arose from the frustration over years of discrimination. Since White Americans had difficulty understanding rap, this speech register gave Black Americans a unique identity and perhaps a sense of superiority that they hadn't felt before socially. By the 1970s spoken rap evolved into hip hop and Latinos also became proficient in this new art form. The music, in turn, lent itself to additional language variations such as slam poetry. By the 1990s, hip hop had evolved into a more militant, anti-social genre in which violence; promiscuity, drug use, and misogyny dominated the music, which represented a particular social cross-section of the population. Now the genre has spread to a variety of applications.

ESOL teachers should be aware of these sociolinguistic functions of language and compare different social functions of language with their students. Knowing and being able to use appropriate registers allows learners to function more effectively in social situations. Learners must acquire the social, as well as the linguistic aspects of American English. Sociolinguistic functions of a language are best acquired by using the language in authentic situations.

Sociolinguistic diversity, which is language variations based on regional and social differences, affects teachers' language attitudes and practices. Teachers must respect the validity of any group's or individual's language patterns, while at the same time teaching standard English. Vernacular versions of English have well established patterns and rules to support them. Making learners aware of language variations leads to increased interest in language learning and better ability to switch among one or more register or dialect and standard English.

ELLs tend to adapt linguistic structures to their familiar culture, modifying specific concepts and practices. Teachers must identify these variations, call attention to them, and teach the standard English equivalent. The goal is not to eliminate linguistic diversity, but rather to enable learners to control their language use so that they can willfully use standard English *in addition to* their cultural variation.

Various functional adaptations of English have great significance to the cultural groups that use them. Attempting to eliminate variations is not only futile, but raises hostility and reluctance to learn English. Stable, socially shared structures emerge from the summed effects of many individual communication practices. Firmly engrained language patterns serve a purpose within the community that uses them.

Unique variations can arise in as limited a spectrum as within a school. New non-standard English words can represent a particular group's identity, or function as a means to solidify social relationships. As long as students recognize that a variation should not be used as if it were standard English, there should be no problem with its use.

Skill 2.2   Demonstrating knowledge of academic discourse

Academic discourse refers to formal academic learning. This includes all the four skills: listening, reading, speaking, and writing. Academic learning is important in order for students to succeed in school. Cummins differentiated between two types of language proficiency: basic interpersonal communication skills (BICS) and cognitive academic language proficiency (CALP). According to research, an average student can acquire BICS within two to five years of language learning whereas CALP can take from four to seven years. A lot of factors are involved in the acquisition of CALP such as age, language proficiency level, literacy in the first language, etc.

Academic discourse not only includes the knowledge of content-area vocabulary but also the knowledge of various skills and strategies that are essential to successfully complete academic tasks in a mainstream classroom. It includes skills such as inferring, classifying, analyzing, synthesizing, and evaluating. Textbooks used in classroom require abstract thinking where the information is context reduced. As students reach higher grades, they are required to think critically and apply this knowledge to solve problems.

Additionally, the language of academic discourse is also complex for English language learners. With respect to reading and writing, use of complex grammatical structures is frequently found in academic discourse which makes it challenging for the learners. Also, passive voice is normally used to present science and other subject area textbooks. Similarly, the use of reference, pronouns, modals, etc is also a common feature of academic discourse which might cause problems for ESL learners. All of these language features of academic discourse help to convey the intended meaning of the author. Therefore, it is necessary to explicitly teach these language features of the text to the students in order for them to become skilled readers and writers.

Furthermore, genre is also an important aspect of academic discourse. It employs a different style of writing that is unique in itself. The organization of a text structure differs according to the purpose of the author, for example, mystery versus romance. Likewise, in academic reading students come across multiple texts that vary in organization and style according to the purpose of the author and the audience in question. Students need to realize the different features of multiple texts to be efficient readers. With respect to writing, students need to determine the purpose of their writing, for example argumentative writing versus story writing.

In short, explicit instruction of these language skills, grammar, vocabulary, and genre should be provided to the students to help them learn academic discourse in order for them to succeed in a school setting.

Skill2.3   Demonstrating knowledge of language variation.

A dialect is a complete system of verbal communication (oral or <u>signed</u>, but not necessarily written) with its own <u>vocabulary</u>, pronunciation, and <u>grammar</u>. Language variations are often associated with specific regions or social groups. Variations of American English may involve pronunciation, sentence structure, vocabulary and expressions. Dialects are influenced by the social context of language usage. Some factors associated with dialectical differences include ethnic background, gender, age, socioeconomic status, and education.

Often people make sweeping generalizations about dialects, categorizing them broadly, such as "a southern drawl" or "a western twang." The term dialect should not be equated with accent alone. Dialects are complex language systems that have a unique set of rules and vocabulary. In the United States there are hundreds of unique dialects. To the trained ear, the speech of Louisiana dialects is significantly different and distinguishable from Texas dialects, for example, even though we might categorize all of these speakers as having a southern drawl. Other dialects show more profound contrast. Comparing upper-class Boston Brahman speech, which sounds formal and closely related to British English, and Black English, which has a completely different tone and vocabulary, the two sound almost like completely different languages. Black English provides a good example of a language system that has well-developed, consistent rules. For example, in Black English the third person singular form of verbs drops the "s" that standard English uses, so the standard English, "She wants that toy." becomes "She want that toy." Black English also drops helping verbs and adds words that previously did not exist in English: "You jivin' me."

Any dialect that has established consistent patterns of sounds and grammar is a legitimate language system. It has no more or less validity than any other language. However, in academia, what is considered contemporary standard English is taught. Certainly within standard English one experiences variations of pronunciation and grammar rules, but overall there is a reasonably consistent set of rules that can and should be taught to ELLs.

In the ESL classroom it is worthwhile to have ELLs reflect on and discuss dialectical differences in their first language. Recognizing the types of differences that exist among dialects makes learners more aware of how language works. It also may reduce the mystery of why they have much more difficulty understanding some people than others.

Language in general is fluid and ever-changing. Change occurs gradually over time, according to how people speak. New words are added, some words drop out of use, and even grammar evolves. For example, over the past 50 years, the past participle of "to get" has gradually changed from "gotten" to "got": I have got tired of waiting. Evolutionary language changes tend to simplify or reduce the language. Social and regional influences on language also have a significant impact. Dialects emerge to adapt the language to the purpose and identity of the speaker. Teachers having an insight on this sociolinguistic aspect of the language will have a deeper understanding of how the language works and will be better equipped to teach Standard English to ELLs.

Skill 2.4   **Demonstrating knowledge of the appropriate roles of written and spoken standard English.**

Written English has always been the focus of the standard variety with grammarians during the eighteenth century. Literacy is the main reason of promoting the standard variety today. Linguists also define Standard English ad *educated English* or as "the set of grammatical and lexical forms which is typically used in speech and writing by educated native speakers" (Trudgill, 1984). Standard English is considered an important variety of English which is normally used in writing, especially printing. Additionally, it is the variety associated with the education system in all the English speaking countries of the world and. Therefore, it is the variety spoken by the *educated people* and taught to non-native learners.

In a formal setting, people normally speak in the standard variety of English. Therefore, it is normally used in conferences, speeches, interviews, classrooms, business functions, etc. According to Perera (1993), some features are easily recognized as non-standard:

- He ain't here. (negative forms)
- They was laughing. (verb forms)
- I want them books. (pronouns)
- He likes the play what I had wrote. (determiners)

However, Perera (1993) also put forward five characteristics that differentiate spoken standard English from written English.

1. Speech contains false starts, hesitations, mazes and incomplete sentences which are quite unlike writing. In addition, much of the speech we listen to (apart from participation in conversations) is actually written or prepared text, such as lectures, sermons, or on television or radio.
2. Speech contains *discourse markers*, e.g. *well, you know, sort of, I mean*. If speech is deprived of these features, then it would sound like a lecture or an address instead of a conversation among equals.

3. Speech depends highly on the context in which it occurs. Where meaning is derived from the situation. This means that face-to-face spoken language does not need to be as full or as explicit as written language. For example, this utterance might be said to a delivery man, *Leave it there; please* as compared to *Please leave the ironing board in the porch, in the corner behind the umbrella stand.*

4. Speech contains characteristic constructions which do not normally occur in writing. For example, increase redundancy makes processing easier for both speaker and listener, such as, *All the people in my office, they can't speak English properly, they can't write English properly.*

5. Speech is on the whole les formal than writing. When we re writing we know it could be read by anyone. However, when we speak we know who we are speaking to and often know them well. Good use of language entails being able to select the right style for the particular context.

Written Standard English, on the other hand, is more formal and explicit in nature. It is used in legal documents, newspapers, books, journals, educational materials, textbooks, etc. It includes features such as word choice, word order, punctuation, and spelling. It is a form of English that is typically used in academic, professional, and business contexts. It is expected of student to follow the conventions of standard English in their written work. It is important for student to learn this variety of English in order to succeed in academic setting. In addition, students need to comprehend and evaluate the information that is provided to them in their daily lives through newspapers, magazines, etc. This helps them aware of the world around them and to be responsible citizens.

COMPETENCY3   UNDERSTAND THE PROCESS OF LANGUAGE ACQUISITION

Skill3.1   Analyzing major theories of first- and second- language acquisition.

Between two and three years of age most children will be able to use language to influence the people closest to them. Research shows that, in general, boys acquire language more slowly than girls, which means we need to consider very carefully how we involve boys in activities designed to promote early language and literacy.

Various theories have tried to explain the language acquisition process, including:

Chomsky: Language Acquisition Device
Chomsky's theory, described as Nativist, asserts that humans are born with a special biological brain mechanism, called a Language Acquisition Device (LAD). His theory supposes that the ability to learn language is innate, that nature is more important than nurture, and that experience using language is only necessary in order to activate the LAD. Chomsky based his assumptions on work in linguistics. His work shows that children's language development is much more complex than Behaviorist Theory, which believes that children learn language merely by being rewarded for imitating. However, it underestimates the influence that thought (cognition) and language have on each other's development.

Piaget: Cognitive Constructivism
Piaget's central interest was children's cognitive development. He theorized that language is simply one way that children represent their familiar worlds, a reflection of thought, and that language does not contribute to the development of thinking. He believed cognitive development precedes language development.

Vygotsky: Social Constructivism and Language
Unlike Chomsky and Piaget, Vygotsky's central focus is the relationship between the development of thought and language. He was interested in the ways different languages impact a person's thinking. He suggests that what Piaget saw as young children's egocentric speech was actually private speech, the child's way of using words to think about something, which progressed from social speech to thinking in words. Vygotsky views language first as social communication, which gradually promotes both language itself and cognition.

Recent theorizing: Intentionality

Some contemporary researchers and theorists criticize earlier theories and suggest children, their behaviors, and their attempts to understand and communicate are misunderstood when the causes of language development are thought to be "outside" the child or else mechanistically "in the child's brain." They recognize that children are active learners who co-construct their worlds. Their language development is part of their holistic development, emerging from cognitive, emotional, and social interactions. They believe language development depends on the child's social and cultural environment, the people in it, and their interactions. How children represent these factors in their minds is fundamental to language development. They believe a child's agenda and the interactions generated by the child promote language learning. The adult's role, actions, and speech are still considered important, but adults need to be able to "mind read" and adjust their side of the co-construction to relate to an individual child's understanding and interpretation.

Theories about language development help us see that enjoying "proto-conversations" with babies (treating them as people who can understand, share and have intentions in sensitive inter-changes), and truly listening to young children, is the best way to promote their language development.

Brain research has shown that the single most important factor affecting language acquisition is the onset of puberty. Before puberty, a person uses one area of the brain for language learning; after puberty, a different area of the brain is used. A person who learns a second language before reaching puberty will always process language learning as if pre-pubescent. A person who begins to learn a second language after the onset of puberty will likely find language learning more difficult and depend more on repetition.

Some researchers have focused on analyzing aspects of the language to be acquired. Factors they consider include:

- Error analysis: recognizing patterns of errors
- Interlanguage: analyzing what aspects of the target language are universal
- Developmental Patterns: the order in which features of a language are acquired and the sequence in which a specific feature is acquired.

Stephen Krashen developed a theory of second language acquisition, which helps explain the processes used by adults, when learning a second language:

The Acquisition-Learning hypothesis: There is a difference between "learning" a language and "acquiring" it. Children "acquire" a first language using the same process they used to learn their first language. However, adults who know only one language have to "learn" a language through coursework, studying, and memorizing. One can acquire a second language, but often it requires more deliberate interaction within that language.

The Monitor Hypothesis: When the learned language "monitors" the acquired language. In other words, this is when a person's "grammar check" kicks in and keeps awkward, incorrect language out of a person's L2 communication.

The Natural Order Hypothesis: The learning of grammatical structures is predictable and follows a "natural order."

The Input Hypothesis: A language learner will learn best when the instruction or conversation is just above the learner's ability. That way, the learner has the foundation to understand most of the language but will have to figure out, often in context, the unknown elements. Some people call this "comprehensible input."

The Affective Filter Hypothesis: People will learn a second language when they are relaxed, have high levels of motivation, and have a decent level of self-confidence.

Teaching students who are learning English as a second language poses some unique challenges, particularly in a standards-based environment. Teachers should teach with the student's developmental level in mind. Instruction should not be "dummied-down" for ESOL students. Different approaches should be used to ensure that these students get multiple opportunities to learn and practice English and still learn content.

Skill 3.2   Demonstrating knowledge of stages and sequences in second-language acquisition in terms of the learners' individual characteristics.

L1 and L2 learning follows many, if not all, of the same steps.

- **Silent Period:** The stage when a learner knows perhaps 500 receptive words but feels uncomfortable producing speech. The absence of speech does not indicate a lack of learning and teachers should not try to force the learner to speak. Comprehension can be checked by having the learner point or mime. Also known as the Receptive or Preproduction stage.
- **Private Speech:** When the learner knows about 1,000 receptive words and speaks in one- or two-word phrases. The learner can use simple responses, such as yes/no, either/or. Also known as the Early Production stage.

- **Lexical Chunks:** The learner knows about 3,000 receptive words and can communicate using short phrases and sentences. Long sentences typically have grammatical errors. Also known as the Speech Emergence stage.

- **Formulaic Speech:** The learner knows about 6,000 receptive words and begins to make complex statements, state opinions, ask for clarification, share thoughts, and speak at greater length. Also known as the Intermediate Language Proficiency stage.

- **Experimental or Simplified Speech:** When the learner develops a level of fluency and can make semantic and grammar generalizations. Also known as the Advanced Language Proficiency stage.

Researchers disagree on whether the development of Formulaic Speech and Experimental or Simplified Speech is the same for L1 and L2 learners. Regardless, understanding that students must go through predictable, sequential series of stages helps teachers to recognize the student's progress and respond effectively. Providing comprehensible input will help students advance their language learning at any stage.

(IT does not focus on the "learners' individual characteristics)

Skill 3.3   Demonstrating knowledge of the learning process (e.g., metacognitive and cognitive strategies0 that are involved in internalizing language rules for second-language acquisition.

Cognitive strategies

Cognitive strategies are vital to second language acquisition; their most salient feature is the manipulation of the second language. The following are the most basic strategies: "Practicing," "Receiving and Sending Messages," "Analyzing and Reasoning," and "Creating Structure for Input and Output," which can be remembered by the acronym, "PRAC."

Practicing: The following strategies promote the learner's grasp of the language: practice constant repetition, make attempts to imitate a native speaker's accent, concentrate on sounds, and practice in a realistic setting.

Receiving and Sending Messages: These strategies help the learner quickly locate salient points and then interpret the meaning: skim through information to determine "need to know" vs. "nice to know," use available resources (print and non-print) to interpret messages.

Analyzing and Reasoning: Use general rules to understand the meaning and then work into specifics, and break down an unfamiliar expressions into parts.

Creating Structure for Input and Output: choose a format for taking meaningful notes, practice summarizing long passages, use highlighters as a way to focus on main ideas or important specific details.

Metacognitive Strategies

The ESOL teacher is responsible for helping students become aware of their own individual learning strategies and to help them constantly improve those strategies and add to them. Each student should have his/her own "tool-box" of skills for planning, managing, and evaluating the language-learning process.

Centering Your Learning: Review a key concept or principle and link it to already existing knowledge, make a firm decision to pay attention to the general concept, ignore input that is distracting, and learn skills in the proper order.

Arranging and Planning Your Learning: The following strategies help the learner maximize the learning experience: take the time to understand how a language is learned; create optimal learning conditions, i.e., regulate noise, lighting and temperature; obtain the appropriate books, etc.; and set reasonable long-term and short-term goals.

Evaluate Your Learning: The following strategies help learners assess their learning achievements: keep track of errors that prevent further progress and keep track of progress, e.g., reading faster now than the previous month.

Socioaffective Strategies

(a) *Affective strategies* are those that help the learner to control the emotions and attitudes that hinder progress in learning the second language and at the same time to learn to interact in a social environment. Socioaffective strategies are broken down into "affective" and "social" strategies. There are three sets of affective strategies: "Lowering Your Anxiety." "Encouraging Yourself," and "Taking Your Emotional Temperature," which are easily remembered with the acronym LET.

Lowering Your Anxiety: These strategies try to maintain emotional equilibrium with physical activities: use meditation and/or deep breathing to relax, listen to calming music, and read a funny book or watch a comedy
Encourage Yourself: These strategies help support and self-motivate the learner. Stay positive through self-affirmations, take risks, and give yourself rewards.

Take Your Emotional Temperature: These strategies help learners control their emotions by understanding what they are feeling emotionally, as well as why they are feeling that way. Listen to body signals; create a checklist to keep track of feelings and motivations during the second-language-acquisition process; keep a diary to record progress and feelings; and share feelings with a classmate or friend.

(b) *Social strategies* affect how the learner interacts in a social setting. The following are three useful strategies for interacting socially: asking questions, cooperating with others, and empathizing with others, which can be remembered by the acronym ACE.

Asking Questions: Ask for clarification or help. Request that the speaker slow down, repeat, paraphrase, etc., and ask to be corrected.

Cooperate with Others: Interact with more than one person: work cooperatively with a partner or small group and work with a native speaker of the language.

Empathizing with Others: Learn how to relate to others, remembering that people usually have more aspects in common than differences. Empathize with another student by learning about his/her culture and being aware and sensitive to the thoughts and feelings of others. Perhaps a fellow student is sad because of something that has happened. Understanding and emphasizing will help that student but it will also help the empathizer.

Skill 3.4   Applying knowledge of the role of the first-language in second-language acquisition and learning (e.g., language transfer, interlanguage development)

Interlanguage is a strategy used by a second language learner to compensate for his/her lack of proficiency, while learning a second language. It cannot be classified as L1, nor can it be classified as L2, rather it could almost be considered a L3, complete with its own grammar and lexicon. Interlanguage is developed by the learner, in relation to the learner's experiences (both positive and negative) with the second language. Larry Selinker introduced the theory of "interlanguage" in 1972 and asserted that L2 learners create certain learning strategies, to "compensate" in this in-between period, while the learner acquires the language. The following are some of the learning strategies of which the learner makes use:

- Overgeneralization
- Simplification
- L1 Interference or language transfer

These practices create an interlanguage, which assists the learner in moving from one stage to the next during second language acquisition. For example, **L1 interference or language transfer** occurs when a learner's primary language influences his/her progress in the L2. Interference most commonly affects pronunciation, grammar structures, vocabulary and semantics. **Overgeneralization** occurs when the learner attempts to apply a rule "across-the-board," without regard to irregular exceptions. For example, a learner is over-generalizing when he/she attempts to apply an "ed" to create a past tense for an irregular verb, such as "buyed" or "swimmed." **Simplification** refers to the L2 learner using resources that require limited vocabulary to aid comprehension and allow the learner to listen, read, and speak in the target language at a very elementary level.

Selinker theorizes that a psychological structure is "awakened" when a learner begins the process of second language acquisition. He attached great significance to the notion that the learner and the native speaker would not create similar sounds if they attempted to communicate the same thought, idea, or meaning. "Fossilization" is a term applied by Selinker to the process in which an L1 leaner reaches a plateau and accepts that less-than fluent level, which prevents the learner from achieving L2 fluency. Fossilization occurs when non-L1 forms become fixed in the interlanguage of the L2 learner. L2 learners are highly susceptible to this phenomenon during the early stages.

- **L1 transfers:** L1 transfer or L1 interference occurs when a learner's primary language L1 influences his or her progress in L2. Pronunciation, grammar structures, vocabulary, and semantics are commonly affected.

- **Simplification:** The practice of modifying language to facilitate comprehension. Researchers disagree on the value of this practice. Krashen believes that simplification aids L2 acquisition. Others believe that lessening authentic texts diminishes L2 learners' ability to comprehend more difficult texts.

COMPETENCY 4   UNDERSTAND INSTRUCTIONAL APPROACHES, METHODS, AND TECHNIQUES IN SECOND LANGUAGE ACQUISITION AND LEARNING.

Skill 4.1   Analyzing the theoretical bases of historical and current instructional approaches (e.g., communicative language teaching, functional-notional approach, content-based language instruction, theme-based language instruction)

<u>The Natural Approach</u>
According to (Krashen and Terrell, 1983) students can improve vocabulary through meaningful interaction. For example, curriculums with games, illustrations, physical contact with objects and/or illustrations, "yes" and "no" questions, as well as "choice" questions, provide opportunities for meaningful context and ways to acquire vocabulary. Whereas a curriculum which requires "passive" listening limits the student's mental stimulation.

The ultimate goal for second language acquisition is to move students from the "listening" mode to the "speaking" mode (Badia 1996). The first two levels demonstrate skills for promoting listening ("yes" and "no" answers being the exception):

- **Level 1:** The primary goal in learning a second language is meaningful and successful communication
- **Level 2:** Students are encouraged to assimilate the language, rather than possess "knowledge" of it

The second two levels demonstrate skills for promoting speaking:

- **Level 1:** "Low" affective factors encourage students to take risks and challenges and promote success in second language acquisition
- **Level 2:** Comprehension and speaking skills are enhanced through vocabulary identified through contextual cues

Willig & Lee (1996) have specified four developmental stages for this approach.

- **Pre-production stage** concentrates on listening comprehension and non-verbal responses from the students.
- **Early production stage** emphasizes an increasing receptive vocabulary and beginning production language.
- **The Speech emergence stage** allows the student to focus on speaking in simple sentences.
- **The Intermediate Fluency stage** encourages the student's ability to engage in discourse.

Total Physical Response (TPR) is a "command-driven" instructional technique developed by the psychologist James Asher. TPR is a useful tool in the early developmental stages of second language acquisition, as well as for LEP students without any previous exposure to the English regardless of the age of the student.

Through TPR, instructors interact with students by way of commands/gestures, and the students respond physically. TPR emphasizes listening rather than speaking; and, students are encouraged to speak only when they feel ready.

After numerous demonstrations by the teacher and classroom students, the entire group can act out a series of commands concerning daily events (such as going shopping, taking a bus, or preparing a simple sandwich).

The three main trends in the **communicative approach** are:

- **Communicativeness:** Activities that use genuine communication of meaning between the participants.
- **Tasks:** Activities that encourage meaningful communication necessary in the carrying out of tasks.
- **Meaningfulness:** Using language in a meaningful context (activity/task) so that the learning process is more efficient.

When engaging in the communicative approaches, activities or tasks can be adjusted to the levels and needs of the ELL. An ESOL instructor uses a variety of instructional methods to communicate with LEP students. Common techniques, suitable for all levels, are:

Contextual:
- gestures
- body language
- facial expressions
- props
- visual illustrations
- manipulatives

Linguistic Modifications (within a "natural" setting):
- standardized vocabulary
- set standard for sentence length and complexity
- reinforcement through repetition, summarization and restatement
- slower speaking pace

Teaching Vocabulary:
- use of "charades," when trying to communicate a word (acting out the word with physical actions or gestures)
- introduce new vocabulary through familiar vocabulary
- utilize visual props, antonyms and synonyms to communicate vocabulary

As the ELL progresses, these techniques are adjusted according to individual or group needs or proficiency levels.

The Language Experience Approach (LEA) is an instructional technique used to encourage spoken responses from LEP students, after they are exposed to a variety of first-hand, sensory experiences (Badia, 1966). LEA develops and improves the student's reading and writing skills by using their ideas and language.

Content-based instruction (CBI) or "Sheltered Instruction" integrates L2 acquisition and the basic content areas of math, science, social studies, literature, etc. The most current research continues to find validity in the following:

- *Learners do not learn L2 through singular instruction in the language's rules; they learn from meaningful interaction in the language.*
- *Learners will gain proficiency in a language, only if they receive adequate input, i.e., speaking and listening start to make sense to a learner when they can build upon previous knowledge as well as understand context and cues.*
- *Although conversational fluency in L2 is a goal, speaking is not sufficient to develop the academic cognitive skills needed to learn the basic content areas.*

The goal in every classroom is for Limited English Proficiency (LEP) students to learn the basic content areas (math, science, social studies, etc.) To accomplish this goal, LEP students must learn an "academic language" which takes from five to seven years (Cummins, 1993-2003), because LEP students typically encounter issues with vocabulary when being instructed in the content areas.

The **Cognitive Academic Language Learning Approach (CALLA) (Chamot & O'Malley, 1994)** assists in the transition from an ESOL driven language arts program to a "mainstream" language arts program by teaching ELLs how to handle content area material with success. CALLA helps intermediate and advanced students understand and retain content area material while they are improving their English language skills.

CALLA lessons incorporate content-area lessons based on the grade-level curriculum in science, math, social studies, etc. The language functions used in the content class such as describing, classifying, explaining, etc. must be acquired by the student. The learning strategy instruction will be given in critical and creative thinking skills so that ELLs develop the ability to solve problems, extrapolate, make inferences, etc.

The **Whole Language Approach** increases linguistic, cognitive and early literacy skills in an integrated fashion by developing all four language skills (listening, speaking, writing, and reading) (Goodman, Goodman, & Hood, 1989). This approach incorporates elements from several instructional strategies to further reading and writing skills. The primary strategy is the Language Experience Approach.

Activating Background Knowledge is essential for material to be meaningful. Material is not meaningful unless it is related to existing knowledge that the learner possesses (Omaggio, 1993). Otherwise, schemas are not activated and the material remains free of meaning according to the Schema Theory of Carrell & Eisterhold (1983). Teachers must include activities in their lesson plans to activate students' previous knowledge on topics being presented.

Skill 4.2   Applying strategies for integrating assessment with second-language instruction.
Portfolios:
Portfolios are a collection of the student's work over a period of time (report cards, creative writing, and drawing, and so on) that also function as an assessment, because it:

- *indicates a range of competencies and skills*
- *is representative of instructional goals and academic growth*

Conferencing:
This assessment tool allows the instructor to evaluate a student's progress or decline. Students also learn techniques for self-evaluation.

Oral Interviews:
Teachers can use oral interviews to evaluate the language the students are using or in their ability to provide content information when asked questions—both of which have implications for further instructional planning.

Teacher Observation:
During this type of assessment, the instructor observes the student behavior during an activity alone or within a group. Before the observation occurs, the instructor may want to create a numerical scale to rate desired outcomes.

Documentation:
Documentation shares similarities with teacher observations. However, documentation tends to transpire over a period of time, rather than isolated observations.

Interviews:
This type of assessment allows instructors to evaluate the student's level of English proficiency, as well as identify potential problem areas, which may require correctional strategies.

Student Journals:
Students benefit from journals because they are useful for keeping records, as well as promoting an inner dialogue.

Story or Text Retelling:
Students respond orally and can be assessed on how well they describe events in the story or text as well as their response to the story and or to their language proficiency.

Experiments and/or Demonstrations:
Students complete an experiment or demonstration and present it through an oral or written report. Students can be evaluated on their understanding of the concept, explanation of the scientific method, and/or their language proficiency.

Skill 4.3   Selecting classroom activities to accommodate the diverse needs of learners and instructional methods.

Student-centered learning instruction has the benefit of catering to students' individual needs, increased student opportunities to perform, and an increase personal sense of relevance and achievement. Furthermore, it leads to fewer teacher-dominated activities where students individually or in pairs or small groups on different tasks and projects that cater to their different ability levels and learning styles. A number of activities can be used to help ESOL in language acquisition.

- Moll (1988) discusses the value of the *funds of knowledge* that students bring to the classroom. These are student's prior knowledge that could be tapped through daily journal writings. This knowledge gained regarding students lives can be incorporated into lessons and content for course work. It also helps in choosing topics that would be of interest to the students and engage them in the learning process. For example, teacher can plan a unit in which students pick an area of the city they want to learn more about. Student research their selected topic and then prepare a report or a project. Parents and family members can also help students and become part of this research.
- Goldenberg (1992) and Echevarria (1995) presented an interactive form of initiation and feedback called *instructional conversations* (IC). The purpose of IC is to create a comfortable and safe atmosphere for the students to express ideas without holding back. In this approach, students engage in extended conversations with the teachers and with each other to promote language development. For example, teacher will say, "Tell me more about..."and "What do you mean by..." and will then restate students' comments, "In other words..."
- It had also been found that teachers who speak with clarity, use gestures, controlled vocabulary, cognates, preteach difficult vocabulary, and tap students prior knowledge were most successful.

- Pairs and group activities are also important in which students can participate and fell valued. In such groupings, students of different cultural and academic backgrounds work together and participate actively. In addition, teachers can at times pair individuals with different strengths, so that students can learn form each other. This also increases the comfort level of the students, especially quiet students and those that have struggling with English. Cooperative grouping also gives opportunities for students to share ideas and information which promotes problem solving.

- Graves (1998) observes that teachers who seem to know each of their students and who take an active interest in them are most successful. They should also be in contact with the parents and involve them in their children's learning.

- Teachers should also model for their students how to think through problems and acknowledge the difficulty of the language acquisition process. It also helps students to see how teaches think-aloud to express, their thoughts, attitudes, feelings, and learning strategies (Brown, 2008). This modeling of learning strategies by experts can show students the processes that underlie expert performance. This modeling can also be done by peers or student tutors that would make the goals more achievable for the students.

- In addition to modeling, teachers should plan instruction so students could experience successful learning and develop independent learning skills. This is referred to as scaffolding where the teacher initially provides sufficient support to practice their newly acquired skills and experiment with the new concepts until they are clear and become part of their learning process.

- Teachers should use *multiple intelligences approaches* to teaching the same lesson. Humans learn in at least seven different ways: visually/ spatially, musically, verbally, logically/ mathematically, interpersonally, intrapersonally, and bodily/kinesthetically. These factors should be kept in mind when planning a lesson. ELLs can benefit from a variety of instructional methods that cater to their different learning styles. For example, the tactile learner can have the opportunity to learn through hands-on activities, increasing the student's learning experience. During such activities, students learn while discussing, investigating, creating, and discovering with other students. In time, students gain background regarding the subject they are learning and start making their own decisions, requiring less teacher support and more student-centered interactions (Cooperstein & Kocevar-Weidinger, 2004).

Skill 4.4   Choosing appropriate instructional practices to achieve curricular objectives

Curriculum objectives are based on the needs and background of the students. These needs of students learning English as a second or additional language has resulted in the increasing demand on all teachers and classrooms to meet these needs of the students, which includes both content and language teachers. Recent research in this area has come up with useful insights which could be applied across both grade level and language classroom settings in order to support ESL students' English language and literacy development. Language and literacy development is the key objective of any grade level curricula to ensure success both inside and outside of the school setting.

These insights can be synthesized into seven key instructional criteria for designing and conducting instruction to support ESL students' language and literacy development (Enright, 1991):

1. *Collaboration:* Instruction should be organized for students to have many opportunities to interact and work cooperatively with each other and with teachers, family members, and community members. During collaborative activities, teachers and students actively work together in order for learning to take place. This entails organizing learning activities which require communicating and sharing, such as discussion groups, student partners or student-teacher dialogue journals. Collaborative activities also include activities that involve students in interacting with people outside of the classroom, such as interviewing the school drama club for the class newspaper or working with a parent or an elder regarding special family tradition.

2. *Purpose:* Instruction is organized so that students have multiple opportunities to use authentic oral and written language to complete tasks and have real life goal and purposes. An example of purposeful composition and questioning activities would be students writing letters to city officials to invite them to a class election forum and then interviewing them about school issues. In addition to this, there are four major kinds of purposeful discourse that can be used as part of learning activities across the curriculum. These are: (a) *shared discourse* in which language is used socially to communicate and share meaning in order to accomplish social goals (playing games or planning a short scene), (b) *fun discourse* in which language is used for fun (singing songs and writing riddles), (c) *fact discourse* in which language is used to get new information and concepts (doing a research project), (d) *thought discourse* in which language is used to imagine and create new ideas and experiences (writing poetry or critical thinking). These discourse features ensure that students learn both language and content with a clear goal in mind.

3. *Student interest:* Instruction is organized to both promote and follow students' interest. This does not mean that the instructional goals are changed but the focus is on organizing activities which combine students' interest and purposes with the curriculum topics and objectives.

4. *Previous experience:* Instruction is organized to include students' previous experiences in to the new learning. This includes tapping students' previous language and literacy experiences in their first language and English and also their already developed knowledge and cultural experiences. This entails relating new concepts and materials to students' background experiences, such as brainstorming ideas before reading a text or connecting previous class activities and learning to new ones. An example would be including histories and folk tales from ESL students' families and native countries in reading group instruction or having students collect authentic speech and literacy data from their homes and neighborhoods to be studied in class.

5. *Support:* Instruction is organized so students feel comfortable and take risks in using English. The classroom atmosphere should be supportive which provides challenging but safe opportunities for students to learn English. The activities are adapted to students' current language and literacy capabilities or *zones of proximal development* (Vygotsky, 1978) in the second language which also provides scaffolding of the newly acquired skills.

6. *Variety:* Instruction is organized to include a variety of learning activities and language forma and uses. This means that students are exposed to a wide range of oral and written English that they are expected to use in the classrooms and their daily lives. This organization of variety includes the instructional practices of collaboration, learning purposes, student interests, and familiar and unfamiliar student experiences within classroom learning activities.

7. *Integration:* Instruction is organized to integrate the various programs and resources available for supporting ELLs' language and literacy development so that they complement each other. This may include integrating the students' in-school and out-of-school experiences; integrating content and language instruction; integrating the four language skills of reading, writing, listening, and speaking; and integrating the students within the classroom through cooperative learning.

Furthermore, Enright (1991) puts forward modifications in *teacher talk* that that could help make language accessible to the students. Krashen and Terrell (1983) refer to it as *comprehensible input* which is *just beyond* ESOL students current language capabilities. There are various ways in which language teachers and content area teachers can adapt their own classroom discourse to make it comprehensible and useful:

- *Nonverbal adaptations:* This includes gestures, nonverbal illustrations of meanings, and facial expressions.
- *Contextual adaptations:* This includes *visual aids* (e.g., pictures, blackboard sketches, real-life objects) and *auditory aids* (e.g., recorded sounds or recorded speech).

- *Paraverbal adaptations:* Teachers speak more clearly, slowing down the rate of their speech, and pausing between major idea units, and vary their volume and intonation to convey meaning.
- *Discourse adaptations:* Teachers use organizational markers, such as now and first, to make their discourse more comprehensible. They also rephrase their utterances and repeat their utterances in meaningful ways.
- *Elicitation adaptations:* Teachers use a variety of techniques to call on students to ensure student involvement. For example, they call on students by name, they call for volunteers to respond, they call on whole group, and they have open elicitations where anyone can speak.
- *Questioning adaptations:* Teachers vary heir questions according to the proficiency level of the students. For limited English proficiency students, the answer could be a sketch or a drawing to one- word elicitation: whereas, it could be more complicated as the proficiency level progresses.
- *Response adaptations:* Teachers adapt their responses to students' utterances to provide further comprehensible input and to encourage further language use by using *confirmation checks* and *clarification requests*. Teachers also rephrase students' responses to provide further information on the topic. Teachers also encourage student response by giving them more *wait time* between the question and the response, through *prompting*, and through *repeating* the response.
- *Correction adaptations:* Teacher correct students' responses by focusing on the meaning conveyed by modeling the correct answer or by explicitly showing the student his/her error and provide corrective feedback individually or away from the group.

The above modifications to teacher discourse are beneficial but it is important that teacher talk does not dominate class discourse. Therefore, learning activities should focus on student collaboration in pairs and groups and independent work. This allows students to receive more comprehensible input from many sources and to use it in many ways.

Skill 4.5 **Demonstrating knowledge of classroom organization strategies to create opportunities for meaningful communication.**

Classroom organization has a significant influence on the language learning process. The second language classroom focuses on a student-centered classroom where students work individually or in pairs or small groups, on assigned tasks and projects. Classroom organization that focuses on learner-centered instruction provides students with greater opportunities to perform productively in the target language, as well as a sense of achievement and personal success.

In general, pair and group work are considered the most effective and meaningful classroom organization techniques. Classroom-centered research has demonstrated that pair and group work gives students a great deal of opportunity to engage in meaningful communication, and they also perform equally well with respect to grammatical accuracy as when the teacher is leading the discussion.

Pair work
Pair work helps students engage in meaningful conversations that lead to the use of language to exchange ideas and information with their fellow student. To promote effective pair work, students should engage in tasks that require exchange of information in order to be successfully completed. Activities like 'Information- Gap' require students to negotiate information in order to complete the task.

Group work
Group work is considered to generate exchange of meaningful discussions (negotiation of meaning) that leads to a greater use of target language which facilitates learning. Studies have found that ELL participating in interactive discussion tasks used a wide range of language as opposed to ELL in larger groups engaged in discussing the same question, with the teacher leading the discussion. The study also suggested that larger groups might cause "students' utterances to be briefer and less complex" while the smaller groups provides a relaxed atmosphere which benefits students language production. A productive group would be of two to five students performing "task-based consensus activities".

Additionally, it has been observed the many students, especially from Asian cultures, avoid speaking in front of the whole class, but are much more comfortable interacting in small groups. Therefore, group work utilizes class time effectively and also produces more complex speech and encourages students to take risk and produce spontaneous speech. This leads to "cooperative learning" where students work together to complete the task at hand. Within a group, students are assigned roles (*leader, time manager, speaker, etc*) to make sure all the members of the group participate.

Whole class cooperative learning

Just as individuals contribute in a group, different groups can also contribute in creating whole class cooperative activities. Different groups produce work that brings forward diverse ideas. These groups can be linked through "different tasks and roles and shared responsibilities to generate whole class tasks and objectives". This approach engages different groups within a classroom to collectively work towards completion of a project. An example would be jigsaw reading where each group is assigned one reading or part of a reading which further requires them to work with other groups to combine their respective parts to make sense of the whole reading.

COMPETENCY 5   UNDERSTAND FACTORS THAT MAY INFLUENCE ENGLISH LANGUAGE LEARNERS' DEVELOPMENT OF ENGLISH.

Skill 5.1   Analyzing cultural and environmental factors that may affect students' English language development (e.g., age, motivation)

Gender influences second language acquisition, particularly of English. Typically, families who immigrate to the United States bring with them their experience of gender roles. Depending on the country, strict cultural norms can diminish the role of the woman, while placing higher regard on the man. Countries such as China value males more than females. If a Chinese family immigrated to the United States, existing sexist attitudes towards the female would still prevail, regardless of the new culture's attitudes toward gender equality. As a result, the family may focus on and only be very supportive of the education of their sons, placing little emphasis on their daughters' education. Many cultures, including many Hispanic countries, value the traditional role of women as mother and homemaker. Many Hispanic families feel that education goes against what they want for their daughters and will not allow them to continue with higher education.

Age can impact second language acquisition, as well, when a culture determines what a person does, as well as when they can do it. For example, as noted by Sindell (1988), middle-class European Americans tend to expect that children will play and behave appropriate to their age, rather than take on more adult responsibilities. In contrast, young Cree Indian children are expected to carry out many adult responsibilities. Furthermore, many Cree Indian parents disapprove of academic activities because they distract the children from involvement in the Cree Indian society.

Motivation: Researchers Gardner and Lambert (1972) have identified two types of motivation in relation to learning a second language:

- **Instrumental Motivation:** acquiring a second language for a specific reason, such as a job
- **Integrative Motivation:** acquiring a second language to fulfill a wish to communicate within a different culture

Neither type stands completely alone. Instructors recognize that motivation can be viewed as either a "trait" or a "state." As a trait, motivation is more permanent and culturally acquired, whereas as a state, motivation is considered temporary because it fluctuates, depending on rewards and penalties. These factors can act as a filter, causing confusion and inhibiting learning. Since language by definition is an attempt to share knowledge, the cultural, ethnic, and linguistic diversity of learners influences both their own history as well as how they approach and learn a new language.

Teachers must assess the ELL to determine how cultural, ethnic, and linguistic experience can impact the student's learning. This evaluation should take into account many factors, including:

- The cultural background and educational sophistication of the ELL
- The exposure of the ELL to various English language variants and cultural beliefs.

Culture encompasses the sum of human activity and symbolic structures that have significance and importance for a particular group of people. Culture is manifested in language, customs, history, arts, beliefs, institutions and other representative characteristics, and is a means of understanding the lives and actions of people.

Customs play an important part in language learning because they directly affect interpersonal exchanges. What is polite in one culture might be offensive in another. For example, in the U. S. making direct eye contact is considered polite, and not to make eye contact connotes deviousness, inattention, or rude behavior; however, the custom in many Asian cultures is exactly the opposite. Teachers who are unaware of this cultural difference can easily offend an Asian ELL and unwittingly cause a barrier to learning. However, teachers who are familiar with this custom can make efforts not to offend the learner, and can teach the difference between the two customs so that the ELL can learn how to interact without allowing contrary customs to interfere.

Occupation, especially in the United States, often determines one's economic status, level of prestige, and amount of power and influence. However, in other countries, regardless of how much one earns, the type of power and prestige available may largely depend on family connections or position within the dominant religious establishment. Learner perceptions of occupations, i.e., whether a certain position is of interest or even feasible, affects second language acquisition. If education is not viewed as a realistic pathway to a career and economic security, then academic success and L2 proficiency becomes less of a priority.

Beliefs and institutions have a strong emotional influence on ELLs and should always be respected. While customs should be adaptable similar to switching registers when speaking, no effort should be made to change the beliefs or institutional values of an ELL. Presenting new ideas is a part of growth, learning, and understanding. Even though the beliefs and values of different cultures often have irreconcilable differences, they should be addressed. In these instances teachers must respect alternative attitudes and adopt an "agree to disagree" attitude. Presenting new, contrasting points of view should not be avoided because new ideas can strengthen original thinking as well as change it. All presentations should be neutral, however, and no effort should be made to alter a learners thinking. While addressing individual cultural differences, teachers should also teach tolerance of all cultures. This is especially important in a culturally diverse classroom, but will serve all students well in their future interactions.

In some cultures, children who learn a second language at the expense of their primary language might be viewed as "turncoats" by family and friends. This can cause negative feelings about school in general and can adversely affect second language acquisition.

Skill 5.2   **Analyzing social and psychological factors that may affects students' English language development (e.g., personality cultural transition)**

Social class or status can also heavily influence second language acquisition, as some countries hold strong beliefs as to whether an individual can rise above their intended station in life. India is a prime example of a highly stratified society. Indians believe in a caste system that prohibits individuals from moving beyond their original social class, unlike in the United States, where the constitution guarantees "life, liberty, and the pursuit of happiness" to each of its citizens. While many people in the U. S. believe education is the key to higher paying jobs and economic security, this sentiment is not embraced by some of the young male population born in St. Croix. They believe that the educational system "subjugates" rather than "educates." These men share a commonly held belief that the social position of their family, rather than academic achievement, ensures economic prosperity and power (Gibson, 1991a.)

Self-Esteem: Learning a second language puts learners in a vulnerable frame of mind. While some learners are less inhibited about taking risks, all learners can easily be shut down if their comfort level is surpassed. Using teaching techniques that lower stress and emphasize group participation rather than focusing on individuals getting the right answer reduces anxiety and encourages learners to attempt to use the new language.

Anxiety: Anxiety is inherent in second-language learning. Students are required to take risks, such as speaking in front of their peers. Without a native's grasp of the language, second language learners are unable to express their individuality, which is even more threatening and uncomfortable. However, not all anxiety is debilitative. Bailey's (1983) research on "facilitative anxiety" (anxiety that compels an individual to stay on task) is a positive factor for some learners, closely related to competitiveness.

Attitude: Attitude typically evolves from internalized feelings about oneself and one's ability to learn a language. On the other hand, one's attitude about language and the speakers of that language is largely external and influenced by the surrounding environment of classmates and family.

If non-native speakers of English experience discrimination because of their accent or cultural status, their attitude toward the value of second-language learning may diminish. Schools can significantly improve the attitude towards SLA by encouraging activities between native speakers and ELLs. This can be mutually beneficial to both groups if students learning the SLA's first language work on projects together. When native speakers get a chance to appreciate the SLA's language skill in their first language, attitudes change and ELLs have an opportunity to shine.

Acculturation is the process of becoming accustomed to the customs, language, practices, and environment of a new culture. The factors that influence this process include, but are not limited to, the learner's desire and ability to become a part of the dominant culture.

The relationship between acquiring a second language and adopting the new culture is a strong one. Schumann (1978a) has developed a model of acculturation, which asserts, "the degree to which a learner acculturates to the target language group will control the degree to which he acquires the second language" (p. 34). Or, put another way, "the level to which a learner can assimilate into the culture, will dictate the level of second language proficiency." According to his model, the following social elements impact the acculturation process:

- The primary (L1) and English language groups (L2) view each other with mutual respect, have optimistic attitudes, and are compatible

- The L1and L2 groups both wish for the primary group to assimilate into the culture
- The L1 and L2 groups agree/accept to share social services and conveniences
- The L1 group wants to remain in the area beyond a temporary status

These factors assist in the process of acquiring English for the L1 group, which facilitates acceptance. Likewise, the absence of these factors can contribute to the L1 group not learning English and remaining outside the dominant culture. In a classroom setting, if there is no mutual respect, positive attitude, or sense of compatibility between the L1 and L2 group, successful second language acquisition for the L1 group is severely hindered. In turn, without a common language, the chances of acceptance and assimilation become significantly reduced.

Classroom and school activities that promote interactions among ELLs and native speakers encourage language growth and an exchange of cultures. With an increased ability to communicate, commonalities are discovered and friendships form. Sports, music, art, photography, and other school activities that allow ELLs to participate while they learn more language provide excellent opportunities for increasing acculturation.

Skill 5.3 Demonstrating knowledge of nonlinguistic and sociocultural aspects of English that are challenging for English language learners (e.g., idioms, nonverbal elements, turn-taking features)

Idioms, particularly those that cannot be translated literally, present a particular challenge to ELLs. Here, again, creating contexts facilitates learning. Grouping idioms according to types of language use helps. Some idioms rely on synonyms, some hyperbole, others metaphor. Having students translate idioms from their native language into English strengthens their ability to appreciate the meaning of idioms. Also, having students create their own original idioms increases understanding.

How idioms are taught greatly affects how well they are remembered and the level of frustration the ELL experiences. Visual representations of idioms make meaning easier to understand and provide a memory cue to prompt recall. Using commercially produced illustrations or having students draw their own representation of the meaning makes learning idioms easier and more fun. Students can also write stories or perform skits that illustrate the meaning of idioms.

Situations dictate language choice, body language, the degree of intimacy, and how meaning is interpreted. For example, when customers walk into bar and sit down on a stool, they expect a bartender will ask them several questions: "What would you like to drink?" and "Would you like to start a tab?" This sequence of events and cues is typical pattern of interaction in a bar. Pragmatic knowledge provides the customer with a set of expectations for the flow of events. Pragmatic knowledge sets customer expectations. Typically people in a bar expect a certain level of social exchange that allows congeniality without intrusiveness. They expect to receive a certain level of service, and to use a particular level of manners. These types of exchanges are fairly universal in bars, but would be completely inappropriate in a more formal setting, for example, when conversing with the president of a corporation.

Vocal discourse varies significantly depending on context. People speak in different registers depending on who they are talking to and what the occasion calls for. A candidate who is running for president and speaking to a group will use more formal speech than when having a casual conversation. The message conveyed may also vary, depending on whether the group is one of supporters or people who hold different political views. In either case, the candidate must make choices about how to organize what he/she says to ensure comprehension and to hold the audience's interest.

Polite discourse includes what is called "empty language" or perfunctory speech that has little meaning but is important in social exchanges. Frequently English speakers start a conversation by asking, "How are you?" even though they have no real interest in the other person's health. An appropriate response would be, "Fine." even if the person may not feel well. The exchange is simply a polite means of starting a conversation. Likewise, at the end of a discourse empty language is frequently employed: "It was good to see you." "Good to see you, too." This type of discourse is considered part of BICS, or Basic Interpersonal Communication Skills, which learners must acquire to function in social situations. It is generally less demanding than CALP, or Cognitive Academic Language Proficiency, and allows learners to participate in informal discourses

Turn-taking: Conversations progress by managing the flow of information back and forth between partners. By taking turns, or alternating roles of speaker and listener, ELLs develop necessary conversational skills. Without these skills, conversations come to an abrupt halt. ELLs can begin by practicing set conversations and progress to initiating and taking turns talking about topics that interest them. Formal and informal conversations must be practiced to prepare learners for the various situations they will encounter.

Skill 5.4   Demonstrating knowledge of the ways in which educational background mat affect literacy development.

Literacy development is affected not only by the individual students' educational background but also by the educational background of their families. With respect to individual ESOL students, it is paramount to note that some adolescent ELLs need to learn to read for the first time, while others are building second or third language literacy with already developed first language literacy (Peregoy & Boyle, 2000). Therefore, those students who lack literacy skills in their first language have inadequate skills to succeed in school and need basic as well as advanced literacy development.

Literacy requires a number of cognitive and metacognitive skills that students can transfer from their first language to their second or third language. In addition to this, students literate in their first language have more *funds of knowledge* or prior knowledge to comprehend the content of the text. The educational background of the ELLs gives them the advantage of transferring their first language literacy skills to their second language and using their prior literacy knowledge to understand the new information (**See Skill 9.2**, focus on reading skills). With respect to writing, research has shown that students who lacked first language literacy strategies displayed a similar lack of strategies for writing in their second language. Mohan and Lo (1985) suggest that students who have not developed good strategies in their first language would not have developed strategies to transfer to their second language. Similarly, transfer of knowledge from L1 literacy help students brainstorm information to help them write about the topic at hand.

Furthermore, family literacy of the English language learners also has an impact on their literacy development. Educational level of the parents has a great influence on literacy development. This leads to the family's attitude towards education and the value they give to success in school. Parents with positive attitude towards education are more involved in school activities and keep track of their child's progress. They attend parent-teacher conferences and are a part of the learning process. Also, parents who read books to children form an early age, and have books, newspapers, and magazines and other reading materials available at home, facilitate their children's literacy development. These families spend time reading together and encourage critical thinking and high order skills in their children. These positive attributes help students develop skills that are critical for success in school.

COMPETENCY 6   UNDERSTANDING METHODS AND TECHNIQUES FOR ASSESSING STUDENTS' PROGRESS IN DEVELOPING ENGLISH COMMUNICATION AND SKILLS

Skill 6.1   Demonstrating knowledge of different types of assessments (e.g., norm- and criterion-referenced, standardized, informal) and important concepts used in evaluating the usefulness and appropriateness of an assessment (e.g., reliability, validity, practicality)

(FL guide does not mention the types of assessments)

Certain factors may affect the assessment of ELLs who are not familiar with assessment in the U.S. or Florida classroom. Among these is unfamiliarity with standard testing techniques. Students may become disconcerted when they are not allowed to ask questions of the teacher, are restricted by time constraints, or are permitted to work only on certain sections of the test at a time.

Students may also be uncomfortable when ELLs are allowed specific accommodation during the test session. Accommodations allowed by the test publisher or those prescribed by the State of Florida need to be introduced in the regular classroom so that ELLs and other students are familiar with them before the testing session begins.

The constructs of reliability and validity are crucial in assessing ELLs because of the high stakes involved in testing in today's schools. Decisions about schools, teachers, and students are based on these tests. A reliable assessment test for ELLs will have the following three attributes: validity, reliability, and practicality.

Validity: An assessment test can only be considered "valid," if it measures what it asserts to measure. If an ELL assessment test claims to measure oral proficiency, then the test should include a section where instructors ask the ELL learner to pronounce certain words, listen to the instructor's pronunciation, and determine if it is correct and/or ask the learner to respond directly to the instructor's questions.

According to Díaz-Rico & Weed (1995), "empirical validity is a measure of how effectively a test relates to some other known measure." There are different types of validity: predictive and concurrent (Díaz-Rico & Weed, 1995.) "Predictive" empirical validity is concerned with the possible outcomes of test performance, while, "concurrent" empirical validity is connected with another variable for measurement. For example, if a learner shows a high amount of English speech proficiency in class, then the instructor would have the expectation that the learner would perform well during an oral proficiency exam.

Reliability: An assessment test can only be considered "reliable," if similar scores result when the test is taken a second time. Factors such as anxiety, hunger, tiredness, and uncomfortable environmental conditions should not cause a huge fluctuation in the learner's score. Typically, if a learner earns a score of 90% on a test that was created by the instructor, then averages predict that the learner probably scored 45% on one half of the test and 45% on the other half, regardless of the structure of the test items.

Practicality: A test that proves to be both valid and reliable may unfortunately prove to be cost- or time-prohibitive. The ideal assessment test would be one that is easy to administer and easy to grade, that includes testing items closely similar to what the learners have experienced in class. However, when learners encounter test items such as writing journals, then practicality becomes an issue. A writing journal, although an excellent method for learners to explore their critical literacy skills, as well as track language achievement progress, can be difficult to grade due to the subjective content, and it may not act as a fair representation of what the learners have encountered in class.

Skill 6.2   Analyzing formal and informal methods of assessing specific dimensions of language proficiency

There are a multitude of tests for evaluating, assessing, and placing ELLs in the appropriate programs. Each test can test a narrow range of language skills (such as discrete tests designed to measure grammar sub-skills or vocabulary).

A language test should be chosen on the basis of the information it gives, the appropriateness of the instrument for the purpose, and the soundness of the test content. Language has over two hundred dimensions which can be evaluated, and yet most tests assess less than twelve of them. Therefore, all language testing should be done cautiously; backed up by teacher observations, oral interviews, and family life variables; and grounded in school records.

Language placement tests:
A language placement test is designed to place a student within a specific program. The school district may design its own instrument or use a standardized test.

Language proficiency tests:
These tests measure how well students have met certain standards in a particular language. The standards have been predetermined and are unrelated to any course of study, curriculum, or program. These tests are frequently used to enter or exit a particular program.

Examples are:

- ACTFL Oral Proficiency Interview (OPI)
- Test of Spoken English (TSE)
- Test of English as a Foreign Language (TOEFL)
- Foreign Service Exam (Foreign Service Institute)
- Oral Language Proficiency Scale from Miami-Dade County Public Schools

Language achievement tests:

These tests relate directly to a specific curriculum or course of study. The tests includes language sub-skills, reading comprehension, parts of speech, and other mechanical parts of the language such as spelling, punctuation, and paragraphing.

Examples are:

- Unit exams
- Final exams

Diagnostic language tests:

These tests are designed to identify individual students' strengths and weaknesses in languages. They are generally administered by speech therapists or psychologists in clinical settings when specific language learning problems are present.

The following are examples of alternative assessments that offer options for an instructor. (informal assessment)

Portfolios:

Portfolios are a collection of the student's work over a period of time (report cards, creative writing, and drawing, and so on) that also function as an assessment, because it:
- *indicates a range of competencies and skills*
- *is representative of instructional goals and academic growth*

Conferencing:

This assessment tool allows the instructor to evaluate a student's progress or decline. Students also learn techniques for self-evaluation.

Oral Interviews:

Teachers can use oral interviews to evaluate the language the students are using or in their ability to provide content information when asked questions—both of which have implications for further instructional planning.

Teacher Observation:
During this type of assessment, the instructor observes the student behavior during an activity alone or within a group. Before the observation occurs, the instructor may want to create a numerical scale to rate desired outcomes.

Documentation:
Documentation shares similarities with teacher observations. However, documentation tends to transpire over a period of time, rather than isolated observations.

Interviews:
This type of assessment allows instructors to evaluate the student's level of English proficiency, as well as identify potential problem areas, which may require correctional strategies.

Self-Assessment:
Students benefit tremendously from a "self-assessment," because through the process of self-analysis they begin to "think" for themselves. Instructors need to provide guidance as well as the criteria related to success.

Student Journals:
Students benefit from journals because they are useful for keeping records, as well as promoting an inner dialogue.

Story or Text Retelling:
Students respond orally and can be assessed on how well they describe events in the story or text as well as their response to the story and or to their language proficiency.

Experiments and/or Demonstrations:
Students complete an experiment or demonstration and present it through an oral or written report. Students can be evaluated on their understanding of the concept, explanation of the scientific method, and/or their language proficiency.

Skill 6.3   Demonstrating knowledge of informal assessment strategies and approaches (e.g., observational checklists)

Portfolios:
Portfolios are a collection of the student's work over a period of time (report cards, creative writing, and drawing, and so on) that also function as an assessment, because it:

- *indicates a range of competencies and skills*
- *is representative of instructional goals and academic growth*

Conferencing:
This assessment tool allows the instructor to evaluate a student's progress or decline. Students also learn techniques for self-evaluation.

Oral Interviews:
Teachers can use oral interviews to evaluate the language the students are using or in their ability to provide content information when asked questions—both of which have implications for further instructional planning.

Teacher Observation:
During this type of assessment, the instructor observes the student behavior during an activity alone or within a group. Before the observation occurs, the instructor may want to create a numerical scale to rate desired outcomes.

Documentation:
Documentation shares similarities with teacher observations. However, documentation tends to transpire over a period of time, rather than isolated observations.

Interviews:
This type of assessment allows instructors to evaluate the student's level of English proficiency, as well as identify potential problem areas, which may require correctional strategies.

Self-Assessment:
Students benefit tremendously from a "self-assessment," because through the process of self-analysis they begin to "think" for themselves. Instructors need to provide guidance as well as the criteria related to success.

Student Journals:
Students benefit from journals because they are useful for keeping records, as well as promoting an inner dialogue.

Story or Text Retelling:
Students respond orally and can be assessed on how well they describe events in the story or text as well as their response to the story and or to their language proficiency.

Experiments and/or Demonstrations:
Students complete an experiment or demonstration and present it through an oral or written report. Students can be evaluated on their understanding of the concept, explanation of the scientific method, and/or their language proficiency.

Skill 6.4 Demonstrating an understanding of sources and causes of potential bias in assessment

Instructors of LEP students need to be aware of the less obvious cultural and linguistic bias in tests, such as students who are unfamiliar with the test-taking techniques of multiple-choice questions and/or bubble answer sheets.

Cultural bias: Concerns acquired knowledge from participating in and sharing certain cultural values and experiences. Asking questions about birthdays or holiday celebrations presumes a middle-class family experience. Immigrants frequently do not celebrate birthdays because they live in poverty or perhaps because they celebrate the birthday differently (with an extended family and piñatas).

The debate as to the "fairness" and/or "cultural bias" often associated with the practice of standardized tests for assessment seems to be particularly true in the case of ELL learners. It has been argued by some that the "very use of tests is unfair, because tests are used to deprive people of color of their place in society" (Díaz-Rico & Weed, 1995.) However, the use of such testing as an assessment tool for ELL learners is standard and will continue to be so, in the foreseeable future. That being said, the following factors can affect how a test or assessment is administered to the ELL learner and should be taken into consideration:

Attitudinal bias: This refers to the negative attitude of the examiner towards a certain language, dialect, or culture. Just as low expectations from instructors can cause low results (the Pygmalion effect), the same thing happens during testing when a negative attitude conveyed by the assessor, teacher, or school culture can have negative results on the test results.

Test bias or norming bias: This type of bias refers to excluding ELLs or different populations from the school's population used to obtain the norm results.
Translation bias: Occurs when the test is literally translated from L2 to L1 by interpreters or other means. The "essence" of the test may be lost in such translation because it is difficult to translate cultural concepts.

Anxiety:
Testing for an ELL may go well beyond what is considered "normal" anxiety for a native English speaker. ELLs are potentially at a much higher disadvantage, because not only is there "anxiety" about studying for a test, the test format itself could be unfamiliar, depending on the ELLs' culture and previous test-taking experience. Multiple choice questions and especially "cloze" or fill-in-the-blanks, can be intimidating, because such formats may not be a true indicator of the ELLs' actual level of ELL proficiency (Díaz-Rico & Weed, 1995.) A potential "workaround" to reduce the ELLs' anxiety would be to administer practice tests, to allow the ELL to develop a comfort level.

Time Limitations:

The time limitations to which L1 learners in the U.S. are typically very accustomed may create issues for ELLs of other cultures, especially in Europe. In the U.S., it is customary for the instructor to assign a class period to complete an exam, or for L1 learners to take statewide school achievement tests, which are timed in a non-negotiable fashion and do not allow the learner to skip forward or back while taking the test. ELLs may need additional time, depending on their comfort level and experience.

Instructor/Learner Rapport:

If the ELL does not share a comfortable relationship with the instructor, and/or there are significant language barriers between them, the ELL may not be forthcoming about any questions or clarification about the test. Without the ability or comfort level to address these issues, the ELLs' success could be compromised before the test begins. Furthermore, nuances of the English language, idiomatic phrasing, and confusing instructions can also negatively impact the ELLs' test performance.

Troublesome Testing Content:

Achievement tests for measuring abilities other than language may contain cultural biases or incorrect translations, which can comprise the scoring for the ELL learner. For example, some words tend to be lost in translation, such as the word "belfry" in English and its corresponding word in Spanish, which is "campanario." "Belfry" is not common in everyday language use, but is usually found in classic literature. However, "campanario" is commonly used in Spanish. The ELL learner's overall achievement on such a test could be greatly diminished by unequal translation.

In addition to the above mentioned factors, cultural and linguistic bias often occurs in tests in other ways.

For example, the story in the English culture generally has a hero and a villain. The leading character is pro-active, assertive, and in search of a goal for which he or she will be rewarded (a pot of gold, the charming prince, or a safe haven). In a Japanese story, the main character's adventures come through chance or fate. His or her rewards come from the kindness or goodness demonstrated throughout the story. Therefore, cultural bias in the story text may lead to testing bias.

The structure of English discourse is usually straightforward. The story starts at Point A and continues until Point Z is reached. There are very few digressions. Many cultures, however, have discourse styles that reflect their culture and are very different. Just as certain cultural amenities (sipping tea as a prelude to business) must be conducted in oral speech, so must they be conducted in writing in certain cultures. To go straight from Point A to Point Z would show rudeness (in oriental cultures which tend to wander) and a total lack of writing ability in Spanish (where the author likes to demonstrate his linguistic abilities through verbosity).

Competency 7   UNDERSTAND METHODS AND TECHNIQUES FOR DEVELOPING AND ASSESSING THE LISTENING PROFICIENCY OF ENGLISH LANGUAGE LEARNERS.

Skill 7.1   Analyzing the role of prior knowledge in aural comprehension

Listening is now not considered a "passive skill" but a dynamic process which makes a lot of demands on the language learners. Keeping in mind the complex nature of processing spoken language, a combination of *bottom-up* and *top-down* approaches have been recommended. The *bottom-up processing* of listening refers to the analyzing of the language by the listener to find out the intended meaning of the *message*.

On the other hand, the *top-down processing* relies on the listener's bank of prior knowledge and global expectations. Prior knowledge allows the learners to predict about the incoming message on the basis of context in which the interaction is taking place. Top-down processing involves prediction and inferencing on the basis of the listener's background knowledge regarding the participants in the situation, their role and purposes, the typical procedures adopted by the participants of the interaction and their consequences.

Educational psychologists found out that verbal learning becomes easier when information can be chunked into meaningful patterns and then related to existing meaning structures in the mind called the *schemata*. Carrell and Eisterhold (1983) discovered that that background knowledge in the listener's mind is of two types: content schemata and formal schemata. Content schemata include familiarity with the topic, cultural knowledge, and previous experience with a field. Formal schemata deals with people's knowledge of discourse forms: text types, rhetorical conventions, and the structural organization of prose. Both content and formal schemata can help listeners in comprehension.

This shows that English language learners should be made familiar with the topic under discussion, the structure and type of text under consideration, and tap into students' schemata and previous global experiences. This would aid the students in listening comprehension and help them develop skills to become proficient listeners.

Skill 7.2   **Demonstrating knowledge of listening skills required in different situations (e.g., listening for gist vs. listening for details, listening to a lecture vs. listening to a context of a conversation)**

Usually when we listen to something, we have certain expectations and a purpose for listening. We have some idea about the content, formality level, etc about the discourse that we are about to hear. Some ideas are based on 'script competence', which is the knowledge the listeners posses in advance about the context or the subject matter of the discourse. These expectations are often linked to the purpose in listening. This means that people listen to specific information or details depending on the purpose of the task at hand (enjoyment, knowledge, persuasion, social or expression).

Listening for gist is to get the general idea or meaning. This means ignoring the detail and just following the overall topic even if you do not understand every word. For example, listening to the news everyday to get the general idea of what is happening in the world. Additionally, if a person listens only for enjoyment or entertainment (like listening to a conversation); he or she will only focus on the overall message.

On the other hand, *listening for details* means to get the specific facts. The focus is to selectively extract information to suit one's purpose. For example, if we want to know the answer to a question then we will expect to hear the appropriate response. Usually, this in turn makes us listen for key phrases or words. When we ask a question like: "Where are you going?", then we listen for the particular expression of place. Additionally, we look for specific information when watching a weather channel to plan a trip or to listen to the sports news to find out the outcome of a game.

Furthermore, *extensive listening* means listening to the overall content of a long text, for example, when watching a film or a play. Likewise, *intensive listening* means trying to understand all the facts and information, for example, for writing a summary or listening to a lecture. However, the skills required might change according to the purpose of the listener. If you listen to a lecture only to gain an overall knowledge of the topic then you will not indulge in intensive listening but will only look for the gist or the general meaning.

Listening purpose is an important variable. The processes and strategies employed by the listener changes according to his or her purpose. Listening to a sequence of instruction for installing new computer software requires different skills and strategies from listening to a poem or a short story. Therefore, when designing learning tasks, it is important to teach students a flexible range of listening strategies and skills.

Skill 7.3   Selecting appropriate classroom listening activities to achieve given instructional purposes

Classroom listening activities are broadly divided into two categories: *Language analysis tasks* (language for perception) and *Language use tasks* (language for comprehension).

Language analysis tasks (language for perception)

The aim of these tasks is to give opportunities to analyze selected aspects of both language structure and language use. It also encourages the development of some listening strategies to facilitate learning. In this category, the actual comprehension is a secondary consideration and emphasis is on aural perception. Activities can focus on one or two points at a time and would include focus on a variety of features of grammar, pronunciation, and vocabulary, discourse markers, sociolinguistic features, and strategic features (Canale& Swain, 1980. Specific activities can include the following:

1. Analysis of some of the features of "fast speech" through the use of tasks that will help students work at learning to cope with rapid, natural, contextualized speech.
2. Analysis of phrasing and pausing points can be used to facilitate listening as well as "chunking" the input into units for interpretation.
3. Analysis of both monologue "speeches" and dialogue exchanges with attention to discourse organizational structures.
4. Describing and analyzing sociolinguistic dimensions, including participants and their roles and relationships, settings, purpose of the communication and its expected outcomes.
5. Describing and analyzing communicative strategies used by speakers to deal with miscommunication, communication break downs, and distractions. (Morley, 1991)

Other activities may include identifying word divisions, identifying stress and unstress, identifying intonation, dictation, repetition, etc.

Language use tasks (language for comprehension)

The aim of these tasks is to give students practice in listening to get information and to use it communicatively. These activities help learners to comprehend and use language in order to communicate effectively. Specific activities can include the following:

1. Listening and performing actions (for example, command games and songs such as "Do the Hokey and Pokey", "May I?" "Simon Says").
2. Listening and performing operations (for example, listening and constructing a figure, drawing a map).
3. Listening and solving problems (for example, riddles, puzzles, real-life numerical, spatial, or chronological problems).
4. Listening and transcribing (for example, taking telephone messages, writing notes).

5. Listening and summarizing information (for example, outlining, giving the gist of a message in either speaking or writing)
6. Interactive listening and negotiating meaning through questioning answering routines (for example, questioning to get repetition of information, questioning to get verification, questioning to get clarification, questioning to get elaboration). (Morley, 1991)

These listening and language use tasks help students to build on their background knowledge in the second language as well as build strategies to facilitate successful communication. In short, all the above activity types help students to develop both top-down and bottom-up processing of information which is essential in building effective listening skills and strategies.

Skill 7.4   Selecting appropriate classroom listening activities that build on and expand students' real-life situations and experiences.

Listening activities used in the classroom should be relevant to students' life and life-style. This pertains to both the lesson *content* (i.e., the information) and the *outcome* (i.e., how the information is used). This is important in order to get learners' attention, to keep them actively engaged in the task at hand, and to maximize the effectiveness of listening/ language learning experiences. Lessons need to present content and outcome that have *face validity* to students. This provides genuine motivational elements for the learners.

It is easy to control relevance if teachers create their own activities. However, in using published materials, only those activities should be selected that are relevant to the particular students. Additionally, it may be necessary to modify the way the material is presented and the way the students are asked to make use of the information. Richards (1983) suggests some ways in which the materials can be adapted: modifying objectives, adding pre-listening activities, changing the teaching procedures for clear presentation, and devising post -listening activities.

Additionally, listening lessons need to have potential for it to be transferred by the learners to out of school situations. Teachers should select specific in-class activities that mirror real-world content and/or outcome patterns so students can apply the skills and strategies applied outside the classroom. An example (of audio and video use) would be for teens and preteen student music videos; the video can be used for listening and evaluating information as well as listening for enjoyment and pleasure and can be applicable to out-of-class music concerts or related peer talk.

In short, the purpose of oral communication in the real world is to achieve genuine outcome. It may be very simple (e.g., enjoying sociable conversation) or it may be very complex (e.g., understanding complex instructions). Therefore, listening activities used in the second language classroom should be relevant to students' real-life experiences and can be transferred and used by students in their everyday situations.

Skill 7.5   Selecting or creating appropriate assessments for given teaching purposes and situations.

Listening is an important skill for English language learners. It is an integral part of communication and need to be taught and assessed effectively. The method used for assessment of listening skills depends on the purpose of assessment. A method that is appropriate for evaluating students at the end of the course is not appropriate to the test taken to give constructive feedback to students engaged in learning a new skill. Moreover, assessment used by teachers should be valid, reliable and fair.

There are different types of assessment that could be used to evaluate students' learning of skills and strategies based on the purpose of the assessment.

Selecting an appropriate instrument for assessment depends on the purpose of assessment and the given situation. If the purpose of the test is to assess a specific set of skills, for example students' strengths and weaknesses at the beginning of the course or students' mastery of a specific skill, then the test should test only those skills. However, if the purpose of the test is to assess distinct goals, then it should measure progress overtime. The use of a variety of assessment tools is important element to consider as well.

Typically, during a listening test, students listen to a passage and then answer multiple-choice questions that assess various levels of literal and inferential comprehension. The important aspects of listening comprehension test are the listening stimuli, the questions, and the test environment. It is important that the listening stimuli should model the language the students are expected to come across in the classroom, in various media, or in conversations. In order to engage the students, the passage should be relatively short and interesting. Furthermore, the topic of the passage should be based on experiences common to all students, that means any kind of bias should be avoided, for example sex, geographic, socioeconomic, or racial/ethnic background.

Additionally, multiple-choice items should focus only on the most important aspect of the passage and should measure a specific set of skills. Students should not have to rely upon prior knowledge or experience to answer the questions. However, an alternative to multiple-choice test is a performance test that requires students to select a picture or perform a task based on oral instruction. For example, students might hear a description of a few scenes and choose pictures that match the description or they might be given a map and asked to follow a route described orally.

Finally, the testing environment for listening assessment should be free of external distractions. If stimuli are presented from tape, the sound quality is of importance. If stimuli are presented by a test administrator, the material should be presented clearly, with appropriate volume and rate of speaking.

Competency 8 **UNDERSTAND METHODS AND TECHNIQUES FOR DEVELOPING AND ASSESSING THE SPEAKING SKILLS OF ENGLISH LANGUAGE LEARNERS**

Skill 8.1 **Accommodating and identifying the instructional needs of students at various levels of oral proficiency**

A necessary first step in planning is to conduct needs analysis which identifies the proficiency level and language needs of the students involved. This helps in modifying and adjusting the instruction, so it could be conducive to learning. Furthermore, attention should be given to the methodology used in class to cover the course materials. With respect to proficiency level, beginning level students require recycling of material from *controlled practice* and *drill* to more *free expression* activities. Whereas, relatively advanced learners may need to polish already developed skills and can be encouraged to involve in less structured activities on their own.

For beginning students, Total Physical Response by Asher (1982) allows Ells to participate without forcing speech in the beginning of their introduction to the English Language. TPR consists of the instructor issuing commands which are carried out by the students. The popular children's game *Simons Says* can be used after the vocabulary items have been introduced in the classroom for a slightly different way to achieve the same goals.

Krashen and Terrell (1983) developed the Natural Approach. Students are introduced to new vocabulary by different experiences. Through listening experiences, TPR uses vividly colored pictures to illustrate concepts. In addition to active involvement with the pictures, learners are able to make choices, answer yes-no questions, and play games. Similarly, the Language Experience Approach (LEA) is an instructional technique used to encourage spoken responses from ELL students after they are exposed to a variety of first-hand sensory experiences (Badia, 1966). LEA develops and improves the students' reading and writing skills by using their ideas and language.

The Cognitive Academic Language Learning Approach (CALLA) launched by Chammot and O'Malley (1994) helps intermediate and advanced students understand and retain content area material as they are enhancing their English language skills. CALLA helps ELLs by giving instruction in the appropriate language areas (specialized vocabulary, syntax, phonology) while dealing with different content areas. Learning strategies that emphasize critical and creative thinking skills such as problem solving, inferencing, etc., need to be taught during these lessons since they are critical to success in the mainstream classroom.

Additionally, it is critical to provide students with comprehensible input which is a level above their proficiency level. For example, for beginning students, this would be in the form of short sentences, phrases, and relatively simple language segments which are integrated into activities of purposeful communication. These exchanges should be as authentic as possible which are carried out in a meaningful context (activity/task). These activities and tasks can be adjusted to the levels and needs of the ELLs. An ESOL instructor can use a variety of instructional methods to communicate with the students. Common techniques which are suitable for all levels are:

Contextual

- Gestures
- Body language
- Facial expressions
- Props
- Visual illustrations
- Manipulatives

Linguistic Modifications

- Standardized vocabulary
- Set standard for sentence length and complexity
- Reinforcement through repetition, summarization, and restatement
- Slower speaking pace

Teaching Vocabulary

- Use of *charades* when trying to communicate a word (acting out the word with physical actions or gestures)
- Introduce new vocabulary through familiar vocabulary
- Utilize visual props. antonyms, and synonyms to communicate vocabulary

As the English language learners progress, these techniques are adjusted according to individual or group needs or proficiency levels.

Skill 8.2   Selecting appropriate classroom speaking activities (e.g., paired and small-group conversations, choral speaking, creative drama, role playing) to meet varied instructional purposes

In recent years, the teaching of speaking skills has moved away from a focus on accuracy towards a focus on fluency and communicative effectiveness. This has affected the kind of activities used by the teachers in the classroom. These communicative activates promote students' ability to understand and communicate real information. It also provides opportunities for them to engage in interaction that is as close as possible to real life situations.

The selection of appropriate activities depends a lot on the level of the learners. For example, the beginning level students need form controlled practice and drills to move to more slightly communicative activities. On the other hand, advanced learners may be asked to engage in less structured activities on their own. Following are the examples of the kinds of activities that could promote speaking skills.

Linguistically Structured Activities

Despite the recent claims, a focus on accuracy is also considered important for language learners. Such controlled activities can be provided with a context, so they could have some of the elements of a communicative activity. This would help the beginner level student focus on accurate structure within a communicative context. An example of this is the *structured interview* where students question each other and answer, exchanging real information while at the same time repeating and producing specific structures (e.g., yes-no, or wh-questions).

Some *language games* can also provide students with controlled practice. However, it is important to model the language structures for the beginning students. Such and other games help students focus on and repeat specific structures as well as perform natural "authentic" tasks.

Performance Activities

In performance activities, language learners prepare for the activity beforehand and deliver a message to a group. This could vary from a student's speech or explain an experiment to simply tell a story from their own experience. The follow-up activity could involve videotaping the students during their performances and having them evaluate themselves. This allows the students to focus on communication on their initial performance and in the follow-up session could deal with specific language features. Additionally, *role play* and *dramas* can be used for all language learners making varying demands on the learners according to their proficiency level. Finally, *debates* can also be an effective performance activity for intermediate and advanced learners.

Participation Activities

Participation activities involve student to participate in some communication activity in a "natural" setting. One of these activities is the guided discussion where the teacher introduces a problem or a controversial topic. Students in small groups discuss the problem and try to come up with the appropriate solutions. For more advanced classes, students could choose their own topic and lead a discussion on it. This activity helps to look from turn-taking elements to topic control among the students as well as accuracy of grammar and pronunciation. Another activity is *interview* where students interview a native speaker about some meaningful or memorable experience in their lives. After the interview, the students organize the information collected to present it to the whole class.

Observation Activities

These are activities in which students records both verbal and non verbal interactions between native speakers or advanced speakers of the target language. This helps students become aware of the language spoken in an authentic setting. It also allows students to observe how people greet each other, make requests, interrupt each other, complement each other, disagree, or receive compliments. A follow-up activity could be a role-play created by the students to show the verbal and non verbal behaviors appropriate in a particular situation.

Skill 8.3   Selecting appropriate classroom strategies to extend students' communicative competence and social interaction skills

To enhance communicative competence, it is paramount to provide students with a relaxed classroom environment in which they feel comfortable and confident. It allows the students to take risks and feel confident to produce more interaction. The teacher should also provide the students with sufficient opportunities to speak as close as possible to real life situations. This provides them with numerous opportunities to learn since the speakers' focus is on the communicative task itself for which they collaborate to achieve mutual understanding and modify their language according to the demands of the situation.

Interactive group work is also important to lessen students' anxiety and lower their *effective filters* which is contusive to learning. Different group sizes (pairs, small groups, and large groups) provide opportunities for students to practice the different thinking and oral skills that is unique to each group type. Similarly, when students' effective filter is lowered, they are more likely to take risks and engage in more meaningful conversations without the fear of mistakes. Students also develop social skills by interacting in a variety of small group situations that aim to resolve a problem or give directions, advice, etc.

In these classrooms, the teacher and students are co-learners whose goal is to communicate meaningful ideas and information. The teacher builds on what the students already know which helps them expand on their prior knowledge and retain information. Also, the questions asked in the class should produce a variety of responses for which there is no right answer. Furthermore, students should be provided with ample opportunities for comprehensible input where meaning is negotiated within a contextualized meaningful context. Some strategies for a communicative classroom could be *peer interviews*, *problem-solving conversations*, *debates*, etc.

Additionally, it is important to provide students with comprehensible input. For instance, for beginner level ESL students, comprehensible input would be in the form of short sentences, phrases, and relatively simple language segments which are integrated into activities of purposeful communication. Similarly, second language learners should communicate in situations/exchanges which are as authentic as possible and should bring about a maximum of personal involvement in the communication. Students should also be provided opportunities to use the target language in social interactions which allow the student to produce the language in a particular context.

Skill 8.4 Applying knowledge of the role of oral language in literacy development

Phonological awareness is a significant part of literacy development in children. Likewise, recent research has shown that phonological awareness also plays an important role as children with limited English proficiency learn to read both in their native language (L1) and in their second language (L2). Students need to understand the words in order to read texts. To read words, they need to be aware of the letters and the sounds represented by letters. This result in the blending of sounds that helps them to pronounce words. Reading educators have found that phonological awareness is critical to the development of comprehension skills.

Furthermore, when fluency in word recognition is achieved, the child focuses more on understanding what is read. Therefore, researchers emphasize the importance of word recognition instruction to enhance fluency. Thus, it is recommended that educators who want to improve students' comprehension skills have to first teach them how to decode well. Explicit instruction in sounding out words is a start in developing good comprehension skills. Word recognition skills must be developed to the point of fluency if comprehension is to be increased.

Recent research has shown that phonological awareness in the native language (L1) of the English language learners predicts successful literacy acquisition in both L1 and second language (L2). Therefore, the closer the phonologies of L1 and L2, it is more likely that the transfer of skills will help the English language learner in their literacy development of L2. Studies suggest beginning instruction for bilingual children with the sounds and patterns that the two languages share. Teachers can then move on to the sounds and patterns that are different in the two languages. In this way, teachers can build upon the transfer of common sounds in both languages in order to help them achieve literacy skills. It could follow with the discussion of the sounds different in the two languages to avoid negative transfer.

In short, phonological awareness in both the native language (L1) and the target language (L2) can help in increasing the literacy skills on an English language learner. It fosters not only their word recognition skills and their fluency but also helps students focus their cognitive capabilities on increasing their reading comprehension.

Skill 8.5 Selecting or creating appropriate assessments for given testing purposes and situations

Assessment of speaking skills should evaluate the communicative ability of the English language learner. It should not break it down into separate categories such as grammar, vocabulary, pronunciation, and fluency. Assessment methods that focus more on the *message* conveyed by the learners are more accurate in evaluating oral proficiency.

There are formal and informal methods to assess oral proficiency of English Language Learners. For example, in the usual classroom setting, students deliver a speech and the teacher gives feedback using an evaluation form. However, more is required than one-time student evaluation and teacher performance of errors and other features. *Peer evaluation* is another method of assessment of speaking skills. For this assessment, the teacher could select two students beforehand to formally evaluate other student's performance. The student evaluator then outlines the main points of the presentation in order to demonstrate the ability to follow the speech. The student evaluator also orally sums up his/her reaction to the performance before the rest of the class. In the end, he/she fills out an evaluation form provided by the teacher for the presenter to read and consider. Other students in the class also fill out the evaluation form and ask the presenter follow-up questions. This evaluation sheet is also used by the teacher foe assessment.

Another method of assessment of speaking skills is *self-evaluation*. This involves audio taping or videotaping students during their initial performances and allowing them to evaluate themselves. Students listen to or watch their recorded speeches and evaluate themselves according to the same criteria that the teacher and peer evaluator use. After that, the student performers select a portion of their talk and transcribe it in detail. In their initial performance, they focus on communication but at this point, they focus on problems and try to make their speech more effective. At this stage, the teacher could focus on both fluency and accuracy so students could understand how both are important for effective communication. These evaluations could b used in various types of classroom activities which helps students gain confidence in their own ability to evaluate language. It also leads to an opportunity for real spontaneous interactions as the evaluation process is discussed among the students and is important to everyone involved.

Apart from these informal methods of assessments, there are some formal methods that are a required to evaluate students in terms of general oral proficiency. There are testing instruments that focus on the *message* produced by the students. Apart from this one time assessments, there are other summative assessments that focus on different types of skills needed to convey the message across by the speaker. For this purpose, many task types are used such as, describe a picture or diagram, give directions, story-telling, opinion-expressing, etc according to the purpose of the test.

Furthermore, *portfolio assessment* intends to examine students' oral abilities over an extended period of time. The purpose is to produce a record of each student's progress on a variety of tasks over the course of a given unit of study. It could also serve as a diagnostic assessment of students' major strengths and weaknesses. These tasks may include describing a picture, oral summary, interviews, information gap, role plays, etc. To create a complete profile of the students' performance, a number of different tasks are included.

In these assessments, it is extremely important that students have the opportunity to practice and be familiar with a particular evaluation technique before being evaluated. Likewise, the teacher should also be familiar with the evaluation criteria of each technique used. In short, a variety of techniques should be utilized in order to evaluate students' overall performance.

Competency 9   UNDERSTANDS METHODS AND TECHNIQUES FOR DEVELOPING AND ASSESSING PROFICIENCY OF ENGLISH LANGUAGE LEARNERS, FOR THE DUAL PURPOSES OF LEARNING TO READ AND READING TO LEARN

Skill 9.1   Demonstrating knowledge of principles of effective reading instruction

Pressley (2008) discusses the mental processes of good readers and states that teachers need to understand what good reading entails. According to him, good readers rely on both decoding strategies and comprehension strategies to achieve their reading goals. The former is called the *bottom-up process* and the later *top-down process*. Both these processes should be taught to increase students' reading ability.

The top-down and the bottom-up processes include the following five components of reading:

1. *Phonemic awareness*: Phonemes are the smallest unit of sound that combines to form syllables and words. For example, the word *shut* has three phonemes (sh-u-t) while *skip* has four phonemes (s-k-i-p). Therefore, phonemic awareness enables the learner to identify and manipulate these phonemes. Some phonemes are absent in students' native language and are more difficult to acquire. In this case, it is necessary to teach phonemic awareness with the vocabulary word, its meaning, and its pronunciation. Additionally, teachers could learn about the phonemes that exist or do not exist in their students' first language in order to provide them with effective instruction. Furthermore, meaningful activities that focus on particular sounds and letters, such as language games and word wall are useful as well as songs and poems that help teach phonemes with rhythm and repetition.

2. *Phonics*: This is the understanding of the relationship between the phonemes and graphemes (the letters and spellings that represent sound in the written language). It helps readers read familiar words and decode unfamiliar ones. Instructional activities that develop students' phonemic awareness help them understand the systematic and predictable relationship between written letters and spoken sounds. Teachers can effectively teach phonics if they have knowledge as about their students' native language. For example, in Spanish the letters *b ,c, d, f, l, m, n, p, q, s, and t* represent sounds that are similar enough to English, so therefore the students may learn then with relative ease. However, vowels look similar in both English and Spanish but are named differently and have different sounds. Therefore, these are more difficult for literate Spanish speakers to acquire (Peregoy & Boyle, 2000).

3. *Reading Fluency*: Reading fluency is crucial for reading comprehension. Fluent reader not only reads words quickly and accurately but also comprehends them at the same time. Students can be taught fluency by reading passages aloud with explicit instruction from the teacher and the other way is for students to read silently on their own with less degree of teacher guidance. However, accent should not be confused with accent as students can learn to read fluently in English even with a native language accent.

4. *Vocabulary development*: Vocabulary development is crucial for reading comprehension. It is difficult for a reader to understand the content unless they know the meaning of most of the words in the text. Additionally, vocabulary development is also important for beginner reading. When a student sounds out a word, it helps to make sense of the word if they already know its meaning and are able to understand the sentence. Therefore, vocabulary needs to be taught explicitly and be a part of the daily curriculum which would help ELLs comprehend academic texts.

5. *Repertories of strategies*: Comprehension is an active process that requires a repertoire of strategies. These strategies help students engage with the text and to monitor their comprehension. Brown (2008) notes that secondary students need a wide variety of strategies in order to tackle the complex reading required of them in order to succeed in and out of school. Students need to be taught explicitly how, why, and when to use these strategies. Pearson and Gallagher *Gradual Release of Responsibility Model* (1983) for adolescence provides guidance with teaching strategies. Teachers become aware of the strategies they use while reading and demonstrate them to the students during think-aloud. Students model these strategies and later adapt them to suit their individual needs. This shifts the focus of responsibility from the teacher to the learner to help them adapt and internalize the strategies.

6. *Scaffolds before, during, and after reading*: Scaffold is the term used for teacher support for a learner through dialog, questioning, conversation, and modeling. A number of such reading strategies like questioning, discussion, and writing are recommended for struggling readers. Roehler and Cantlon (1997) identified five types of scaffolding: (a) offering explanations, (b) inviting student participation, (c) verifying and clarifying student understandings, (d) modeling of desired behaviors, and (e) inviting students to contribute clues for reasoning through an issue or problem. Additionally, these reading strategies/ scaffolding activities should also be used in content-area classroom in order for them to be effective.

7. *Knowledge about the learners*: Diagnostic assessment is necessary to determine the strengths and weaknesses of the students to provide effective instruction. Knowledge regarding the history of students' reading difficulties would help teacher focus more on those areas and also strengths can help support these problematic areas. Similarly, knowledge regarding the cultural and linguistic background of the students assists the teacher in selecting reading material for the class in accordance with their interests, cultural sensitivity, and acknowledgement of their cultural beliefs and values.

Skill 9.2   **Demonstrating knowledge of the transferability of first-language literacy skills into English**

Children learn to read only once. If they are able to read in their native language, they are able to read in English. It is important for ELLs to increase their vocabulary and knowledge of the structure of English, their second language. By building on what the ELL already knows with regards to literacy, language, and experiences in his or her native language, teachers will be able to improve the reading level of the ELL in English. For this reason, it is necessary to evaluate the ELL in his or her first, native, or heritage language in order to initiate the best reading instruction in English.

Teachers can also use the similarities and differences of the different languages to teach learning strategies. For example, the adjective comes before the noun in English but in Spanish it comes after the noun. A text written in English is expected to have a main idea and several supporting details to explain or support it. Other languages are more descriptive and depend on the beauty of the language to convey the writer's meaning. By using the concept of cognates, both true and false, teachers can improve vocabulary development.

Schumm (2006) emphasizes that not only are the reading levels characteristics important, but also the differences between L1 and L2, because these may influence the assumed level of the student. Some of the questions she proposes to elicit these similarities and differences are for further evaluation of reading level characteristics:

- Is the L1 writing system logographic like Arabic, syllabic like Cherokee, or alphabetic like English and Greek?
- How does the L1 syntax compare with the L2 syntax?
- Are the spelling patterns phonetic with consistent grapheme-phoneme relationships (e.g. Spanish or French) or are there multiple vowel sounds (e.g. English)?
- Do students read from left to right and top to bottom in their L1?
- Are there true cognates (Spanish *instrucción* and English instruction) and false cognates (Spanish *librería* <bookstore> and English library) that will help or confuse the ELL?
- Are the discourse patterns and writing styles of L1 and L2 similar or different?
- Are questions with known answers asked (teacher questions) or are rhetorical questions (found among many working class families) asked?
- Is L1 writing style circular, with long sentences and many details (e.g. Spanish) or linear, with the minimum number of facts or supporting details needed to support the main idea (e.g. English)?

Skill 9.3   Identifying strategies that help English language learners utilize their spoken English to develop their reading proficiency in English (e.g., language experience approach)

Fluency is developed over time through extensive practice both in speaking and in reading. Ample opportunities should be given to ELLs to develop their speaking abilities and listening abilities to help them achieve more oral fluency. Role plays, skits, poems, singing, and telephone dialogs are good ways to increase oral fluency. Fluency in reading interacts with oral fluency. Wide exposure to print and reading will increase both reading fluency and oral fluency. The two are intertwined.

Fluent readers are able to grasp chunks of language, read for meaning and not word by word, decode automatically, and are confident readers who are able to self-monitor, but maintain comprehension. Specific instruction devoted to these areas should improve fluency rates in slower readers.

Skill 9.4   Demonstrating knowledge of the interrelationship between decoding and comprehension in English

Teaching decoding skills is considered one of the effective methods of reading instruction. The emphasis is on teaching the phoneme-grapheme correspondences. In order to develop effective reading skills, student should aim *automaticity* i.e. the brain process of decoding letter sound becomes automatic. This leads to fluent reading where the brain may process many letters, sounds, and words at the same time. This is positively related to students' achievement in reading as once decoding skills is mastered, the more attention can be given to master the overall meaning of a phrase or sentence (comprehension). However, students still need explicit instruction in developing strategies to improve their comprehension skills.

Therefore, phonics and other linguistic approaches to teaching reading are important in terms of word identification skills. This accurate and rapid word recognition skill leads to fluency in reading which is considered one of the five critical components of the reading process (National Reading Panel). When the reader's decoding skills become automatic, s/he is able to focus attention on constructing meaning. For readers who have not yet reached automaticity of decoding skills, reading is a slow, laborious, and a struggling process. Fluent readers are more likely to engage in extensive reading as compared to struggling readers. The view that if reader read more, they would achieve fluency is not applicable for ESL learners. Expert teacher guidance is necessary for learners to reach fluency. Several studies have focused on the type of instruction that would increase fluency in readers. These instructional practices include:

- Modeled reading
- Repeated reading of familiar text
- Wide independent reading
- Coached reading of appropriately selected materials
- Chunking of text

- Word reading practice

Even though fluency is an important part of reading, it is in itself not sufficient to insure high levels of reading achievement and comprehension. Fluency is based on foundation of oral language skills, phonemic awareness, familiarity with letter forms, and efficient decoding skills. In short, a combination of instruction in decoding and reading comprehension is required for students to achieve high level of reading skills.

Skill 9.5   Applying knowledge of schema theory in reading instruction

Schemata need to be activated to draw upon the previous knowledge and learning of the ELL especially when the ELL may not have had similar experiences to the mainstream culture. The use of graphics to encourage pre-reading thought about a topic (e.g. brainstorming, web maps, and organizational charts) activates this knowledge and shows how information is organized in the students' minds. Schumm (2006) states that research has shown:

- More prior knowledge permits a reader to understand and remember more (Brown, Bransford, Ferrara, & Campione, 1983).
- Prior knowledge must be activated to improve comprehension (Bransford & Johnson, 1972).
- Failure to activate prior knowledge is one cause of poor readers (Paris & Lindauer, 1976).
- Good readers accept new information if they are convinced by an author's arguments. Likewise, they may reject ideas when they conflict with a reader's prior knowledge (Pressley, 2000).

Skill 9.6   Applying knowledge of various literacy genres and purposes for reading

Critical literacy is the process of in-depth text analysis, in which the learner seeks an understanding, application, and synthesis of the material, including the intentions and resources of the author or speaker, which reaches well beyond the surface meaning (Lohrey, 1998.) According to Van Duzer & Florez (2001), "Critical literacy takes learners beyond the development of basic literacy skills such as decoding, predicting, and summarizing and asks them to become critical consumers of the information they receive."

There is no "correct" or "preferred method" for critical literacy—how it is approached and analyzed, depends on the style, thought processes, perspective and pedagogies of the reader or listener. For example, because the use of language is hardly impartial; there are readers who use critical literacy to explore the relationship between power and language. And, there are those who believe that written or spoken text, be it from a speech, interview newspaper, magazine, internet site, or research book is meant to convince, rationalize, amuse, etc., and, so for those individuals, critical literacy is almost an "investigation" into the motivation and goals of the author or speaker.

Some theorists of critical literacy, such as Freire, maintain that knowledge and education give power to individuals who live under oppressive conditions (Peyton & Crandall, 1995.) Through the process of analysis and investigation, critical literacy provides a means for individuals to identify the nature of social conditions and find a means to change them (Auerbach, 1999; Brown, 1999; Hammond & Macken-Horarik, 1999, Hull, 2000.)

Spoken or written words typically assume that the listener or reader has background knowledge and/or experience particular to a certain culture and its generally accepted norms, values, and attitudes. Thus, instruction in critical literacy is of enormous benefit for L2 learners, as they learn about a new culture by the simple process of questioning it.

Literary genres are collections of works with a similar theme or style. Some literary genres come under the huge umbrella of biography and nonfiction whereas others like folktales are further classified into fables, tall tales, fairy tales, and myths. Additionally, under fiction, three are other literary genres: historical fiction, mystery, realistic fiction, fantasy, science fiction, etc. Students should be made aware of these different genres and the different format and style that make them distinct. This increase in students' background knowledge will help them successfully comprehend the text and build their schemata.

Furthermore, the concept of genre and its purpose becomes more complicated as children advance to a higher grade level. According to Shanahan (2008), people make decisions based on information that comes from multiple viewpoints in multiple formats (e.g., letters, essays, reports, advertisements, lectures) through various medians (e.g., newspapers, television, websites, books, magazines). This is evident in content-area subjects as well. For example, historians supply evidence from multiple sources (e.g., film, newspapers, letters, interviews, fictional accounts) to prove their point of view regarding a historical event. The views regarding a particular event might changes based on the era in which historians were doing the writing and who the historians were. Historians not only read multiple genres when collecting information, but also write them (e.g., scholarly books, journals, articles, lectures). This is true for other disciplines like science and mathematics.

These multiple genres, within a single topic, make reading even more challenging for ESL learners. This struggle is magnified when these genres communicate contradictory purposes and messages depending on the author and the context. These genres and their purpose of writing changes across disciplines; therefore, teachers need to make students aware of these differences so they can become critical readers. Shanahan (2008) suggests what teachers could do to help the students:

- Preteach potentially troublesome vocabulary.
- Have students read an easier text, or to provide information to build background knowledge, use an anchor text or experience before reading a more difficult text.
- Teach students to use strategies that will help them to better interpret the texts.
- Teach students about various genres and structures used in particular texts and how texts within those genres signal important information.
- Teach students information about the discipline in which they are reading__ about how experts in that disciplines approach and use information in text to build upon existing knowledge.
- Set up cooperating grouping structures that allow students who are weaker readers to be supported in their reading by a better reader; one of the online translation site could be used to translate text to a student's primary language.
- Find easier texts or alter existing texts to make them easier; if the difficult texts are so challenging that students become unmotivated, even with all of the support they receive.

Skill 9.7 Selecting and adapting appropriate classroom activities for given instructional purposes and for English language learners for different literacy levels and English language proficiency levels

The instructor can integrate the following strategies to promote critical literacy for L2 learners:

- Ask the L2 learners to consider the author's motivation for writing a certain newspaper or magazine article. Specifically, ask the learners to support their opinions and answers, using examples of tone, structure, and word choice.

- Ask the L2 learners to compare/contrast the photographs, topics, writing style of an L1 and L2 newspaper. Specifically, ask the learners what the style of each reveals about the different cultures, whether these differences influence readership, as well as if the choice of advertising influences readership.

The critical piece of both activities is for the learners to not only consider the specific questions, but to also consider which values, ethics, and cultural factors influence their own thinking and responses.

Most importantly, instructors need to introduce topics that are relevant to the L2 learner, as well as use codes. "Codes" are graphics, pictures, speeches, themes, issues, or realia—objects from a specific culture that help stimulate discussion. "Simple, familiar, focused representations of complex, often emotionally charged issues or situations, codes can be structured for use with low level learners" (Van Duzer & Florez, 2001.) The following is an example of how an instructor might use codes to and facilitate a "critical" discussion: Have the L2 learners watch a clip from the movie "Guess Who's Coming to Dinner?" whose basic theme is racial acceptance and whether a wealthy young college girl's parents will accept her African-American fiancé. After viewing the clip, the instructor might ask the following types of questions:

- *How do you think both sets of parents handled the situation?*
- *If you would have handled it differently, what would you have done and why?*
- *How would your family react, if this happened to you?*
- *Is it possible that this situation could happen to you? Why or why not?*
- *Is this racially-based theme still common on television and in the movies?*

Such questions provide a framework for L2 students to examine their individual values, morals, and biases, as well as society's.

Other resources include **graphic organizers** which help students visualize raw data. These can be used by the teacher for simplification of complex materials, numerous data, and complicated relationships in content areas. Students to analyze data, organize information, and clarify concepts. Examples are: pie charts, flow charts, bar diagrams, Venn diagrams, family trees, spider maps, organizational charts, and strip maps.

Still other graphic organizers are webbing, concept mapping, passwords and language ladders, and brainstorming.

- With **webbing**, students learn to associate words or phrases with a topic or concept.
- By using **concept maps**, students learn the relationships between the different elements of a topic and how to organize them from the most general to the most specific. This is different from webbing where relationships between words or phrases are shown, but not ranked.
- **Passwords and language ladders** are motivating ways to teach chunks of language to ELLs. The "password" of the day is language needed for daily student life in school. After the words or phrases are explained, they are posted on the board, and must be used before leaving the room or participating in some activity. Language ladders are associated words such as different ways to say hello or good-bye.

- **Brainstorming** consists of students contributing ideas related to a concept or problem-centered topic. The teacher initially accepts all ideas without comment. Students then categorize, prioritize, and select proposed selections for further investigation.

Vocabulary

Research has shown that the same 1000 words (approximately) make up 84 percent of the words used in conversation and 74 percent of the words in academic texts (*The Nation*, 2001). The second most frequently used 1000 words increases the percentages to 90 percent of the words used in conversation and 78 percent used in academic texts. The ELL needs to understand 95 percent to achieve comprehension of the academic text. (Lists may be found at: http://www.harenet.ne.jp/~waring/vocab/index.html.) ELLs need to acquire the 2000 most used words and work on academic content words at the same time. In order to help students acquire the vocabulary they need for school, consider the following.

- Vocabulary development for young children is increased using the same methods used with native speaker beginning readers: ample exposure to print, word walls, realia, signs on objects around the room, and so on.
- Older children may take advantage of all these methods in addition to studying true and false cognates, creating personal dictionaries, journal writing between themselves and their teacher, and using learning strategies to augment their vocabulary.
- Other strategies from Peregoy and Boyle (2008) are:

  o Activate the prior knowledge of the ELL
  o Repeat the new word in meaningful contexts
  o Explore the word in depth through demonstrations, direct experience, concrete examples, and applications to real life
  o Have students explain concepts and ideas in writing and speaking using the new words
  o Provide explicit strategy instruction so that students can independently understand and use the new words

Many people wait for a reading passage to present the information in an organized way for them. However, **reading comprehension** is a highly complex area where successful readers use reading strategies in each of the three distinct phases of reading—pre-reading, reading, and post reading—to successfully understand a text (Peregoy and Boyle, 2008).

- The purposes of the pre-reading phase are for teachers to build background knowledge through anticipation guides or field trips, motivate the reader with structured overviews or films, and establish the purpose using experiments or pictures.

- The purposes of the during-reading phase are to read based upon the established purpose using learning logs or annotating texts to record information, improved comprehension by Directed Reading-Thinking Activities and asking questions, and utilize background knowledge by studying headings and subheadings and answering questions.

- The purposes of the post reading phase are to help the student with organizing and remembering information through activities such as art work, maps, or summaries and to use the information in reporting, making a film, or publishing.

Skill 9.8   Selecting or creating appropriate assessments for given testing purposes and situations

Hughes (1989) presents a framework for testing reading abilities of language learners which includes Content (operations, types of text, addresses, and topics) and Criterial levels of performance.

Content

Operations: Operations include different levels of analysis that requires attention. These are the set of macro-skills that covers the objectives of the course and the needs of the students. These include:

- Identifying stages of an argument
- Identifying examples in support of an argument
- Scanning text to locate specific information
- Skimming text to obtain the gist

These also include micro-skills such as:

- Using content to guess meaning of unfamiliar words
- Identifying referents of pronouns, etc.
- Recognizing indicators in discourse, especially for the introduction, development, transition, and conclusion of ideas

There should be a balance of the macro and micro skills tested which should reflect the relationship between the two levels of skill.

Types of text: The designer of the test should identify the type of text used for the test, such as textbook, novel, magazine, newspaper, academic journal, letter, poem, etc. Additionally, the use of authentic texts depends in part on what it is intended to measure. It is possible to use authentic text at lower levels of abilities.

Addresses & Topics: This is related to test types and specifies the audience of a particular type of text. The range of topics can be mentioned in general terms.

Setting criterial levels of performance: In norm-referenced approach to testing, student performance is evaluated by comparison with each other. In criterion-referenced approach, it is specified what the candidate should know to achieve a specific level. However, this could be difficult with reading to provide interpretations of scores (e.g. what does a student know if s/eh gets 60 or 70%). It would be best to use the test task itself to define the level (Hughes, 1989). For example, in order to pass the student should be able to score a particular number of items correct (say 80 per cent). Additionally, while scoring, errors of grammar, spelling or punctuation should not be penalized if the student is able to successfully complete the task.

Setting the tasks

Selecting the texts:
- Keep the content and the criteria level in mind when selecting a text.
- Choose text of appropriate length. For example, scanning may require a longer passage (approx. 2000 words) as opposed to detailed reading.
- To obtain reliability, include as many passages as possible in order to give candidates ample chances to show performance level.
- Choose a text of interest to the students.
- Texts should be avoided that contain information that is part of the students' general knowledge which would enable them to answer questions without reading the passage.

Writing items

The purpose of the test items should be to elicit reliable performance of successful reading and to achieve reliable scoring. They should be within the capabilities of the students and should make minimal demands on their writing skills. Those items should be avoided for which the correct response can be found without understanding the text. Also, paragraph numbers and line numbers should be added to the text if items need to make reference to them. It is very important to get the opinion of colleagues on the text and the test items.

Possible Techniques: The items should interfere as little as possible with the reading itself and it is also avoid asking students to write answers in response to the reading passage. Some of the methods used are:

- Multiple choice: Students are provided with choices from which they choose the correct answer. True/False questions are also a variety of multiple choice.
- Unique answer: In this task type, there is only one possible correct answer. This might be a single word or number, or something a little longer. The test item may be a question: however, this form is not recommended to be used extensively.

- Short answer/Guided short answers: Short answers can be used when unique answer items are not possible. However, it may again be the problem that student might not be able to express themselves through writing. Therefore, it is possible to provide partial information to the students where they have only to complete sentences already given to them. For example: "Many universities in Europe used to insist that their students speak and write only _____. Now many of them accept _____ as an alternative, but not a _____ of the two." Hughes (1989)
- Summary cloze: In this technique, a reading passage is summarized and gaps are left in the summary for students to complete. Similar to guided answers, this is a more reliable way of testing reading.
- Information transfer: Another way of limiting the demands on students writing ability is to ask them to perform successful completion of a reading task is transferring simple information in different ways, such as a table, following a route on a map, labeling a picture, or number a series of events etc.

Competency 10   UNDERSTAND METHODS AND TECHNIQUES FOR DEVELOPING AND ASSESSING THE WRITING SKILLS OF ENGLISH LANGUAGE LEARNERS

Skill 10.1   Analyzing the role of other communicative modes (e.g., speaking, reading) in developing the writing skills of English language learners

Integration of all four skills is beneficial for all English language learners regardless of their proficiency level (Genesee et. al., 2006).   This provides a framework for the learners where they can exercise their wiring skills. The integration of the four skills provides an effective context for writhing so that the use of one leads naturally to the use of another as in real life. In this way, the learners will see how writing relates to certain communicative needs just as the other skills. For example, students need to participate in classroom conversations by articulating their opinion, sharing their observations, making comparisons, etc. through speaking and writing. They need to listen to the topic, take notes, discuss with their classmates, and read about the topic which requires the integration of all four skills.

If the learners need to engage in real-life communicative situations, then the activities should be organized in a way to make them use all four language skills. In order to do this, the students should not only speak with the teacher but also with other students. This means that the student will also listen and try to comprehend what the speaker is saying. The listener can then react by writing down for a reader his version of the information he had just heard. This sequence of activity helps students brainstorm ideas in the target language before they put it on paper. There is thus very little opportunity for the student to translate his idea form his/her native language into English.

In this case, prewriting techniques give the students opportunity to use all the four skills to help them explore and get started with their ideas on a given topic or to develop a topic for a writing activity based on communicative classroom activities.

- *Brainstorming*
  Brainstorming lets students work together in the classroom in small groups to say as much as they can about a topic. This helps them generate ideas to use for their individual brainstorming on paper. This activity involves the use of both speaking and listening skills to produce effective writing.

- *Guided Discussion*
  Another way to get students talk about a topic or to focus on specific aspects of a topic is to provide guidelines for group or whole class discussion. This technique has the advantage of helping the students beforehand with the vocabulary and sentence forma that they might need in their discussion. This again makes the use of all the four skills to guide students in their writing process.

Some of the other activities that make students use their other linguistic skills are:

- Interviews
- Skits
- Dictation
- Note-taking
- Story-telling

Skill 10.2   Applying knowledge of the writing process in designing activities to develop students' writing proficiency.

Just as the native English speaker has to manage many different skills to become a proficient writer, so must the ELL student including clarity of thought and expression, how to use different genres to convey different purposes in writing as well as conventional spelling, grammar, and punctuation. Since these skills vary in addition to the traits of each specific type of writing, it is not easy to discuss writing stages. Even so, it is important for teachers to have a general guide on which to base their instruction plans.

The following chart, based on a Writing Matrix developed by Peregoy and Boyle (2008), offers a good guide to identifying characteristics of a student's writing level. It encompasses three developmental levels and six traits.

- Trait 1: Fluency
  Beginning Level: Writes one or two short sentences.
  Intermediate Level: Writes several sentences.
  Advanced Level: Writes a paragraph or more.

- Trait 2: Organization
  Beginning Level: Lacks logical sequence or so short that organization presents no problem.
  Intermediate Level: Somewhat sequenced.
  Advanced Level: Follows standard organization for genre.

- Trait 3: Grammar
  Beginning Level: Basic word-order problems. Uses only present tense form.
  Intermediate Level: Minor grammatical errors.
  Advanced Level: Grammar resembles that of native speaker of same age.

- Trait 4: Vocabulary
  Beginning Level: Limited vocabulary. Needs to rely at times on L1 or ask for translation.
  Intermediate Level: Knows most words needed to express ideas but lacks vocabulary for finer shades of meaning.
  Advanced Level: Flexible in word choice; similar to good native writer or same age.

- Trait 5: Genre
  Beginning Level: Does not differentiate form to suit purpose.
  Intermediate Level: Chooses form to suit purpose but limited in choices of expository forms.
  Advanced Level: Knows several genres; makes appropriate choices. Similar to effective native writers of same age.

- Trait 6: Sentence variety
  Beginning Level: Uses one or two sentence patterns.
  Intermediate Level: Uses several sentence patterns.
  Advanced Level: Uses a good variety of sentence patterns effectively.

In the beginning, the focus of research was on the product produced by the writer. However, Emig's (1971) L1 research changed the focus from product to process. This has become the focus of the research design for conducting research in both L1 and L2 writing process. Similar to Emig's research, L2 composition specialist Zamal (1976) and Raimes (1979) recommended treating L2 writing as a process in the L2 classroom which focuses less on surface-level errors and achieving correctness but stress more on process-oriented pedagogy. In a process-oriented writing class, the teacher provides students with a wide range of strategies for composing texts. This approach focuses on what the writer does (planning, revising, etc) instead of only what the final product look like (grammar, spelling, etc).

The goal of a writing class is to have ESL students write essays that match the level of content and skills of a native speaker, but this is not possible at the beginning or intermediate-level language learners. One approach that addresses these developmental stages is to characterize writing tasks along a continuum from *controlled* to *guided* to *free* which starts with maximum teacher controlled activities to tasks that require students to supply content, organization, and language structure. A common kind of controlled writing is to give a paragraph in which students are asked to change a given feature, such as verb tense, which requires other changes in the text, such as time reference. An example of a guided writing task, which allows more freedom to the student than controlled task, is to ask students to produce a short text by answering directed yet open-ended questions. Finally, free writing tasks ask students to produce complete texts in response to a variety of writing tasks. Free writing can also be encouraged with less emphasis on the correctness on grammar or of form by having student keep a journal.

The focus of every writing class should be to allow students to learn and practice the skills of producing good writing. Regardless of the kind of writing task, prewriting is important at the beginning. The goal of the teacher should be to present students with a variety of prewriting strategies and help them figure out which on works best for them. Some examples are:

- Brainstorming
- Listing
- Free writing
- Clustering

After this first step, the teacher need to make students produce a number of drafts on their written task, especially at the *free writing* stage. This is an essential part of the writing process where students need to learn to revise and to work through a series of drafts before considering a paper finished.

Another stage that requires a lot of attention is the *responding* to student writing. This is a complex process which requires teachers to develop or adopt strategies which help foster student improvement. Moreover, students should also be trained to use the feedback in ways that will improve their writing. This feedback should not only be on surface level errors but on the relevance of the idea to the topic and also on strategies students should utilize in producing better essays. These strategies should be taught explicitly to the students (prewriting, revising, organizing, etc) for them to implement during the writing process. There are many ways of teacher feedback:

- *Oral teacher feedback* in the form of individual or group conferences.
- *Peer response* in which students read or listen to each other papers for the purpose of providing insight. This could be done both in groups or pairs. Teacher can provide guidelines to the students so they remain focus on the task at hand.

The above stages are important in the writing process and should be implemented effectively by the teacher. The writing of the composition as well as the feedback stage of the writing process is crucial in improving the writing abilities of ESL learners.

Skill 10.3   Identifying strategies for developing students' organization in writing and the ability to write in different academic genres (e.g., narration, analysis)

The organization of written discourse in English is culturally determined; therefore, students who write well in their first language cannot simply rely solely on their prior writing skills. Students have to learn not only how English sentences are formed but how paragraphs and longer pieces are constructed. In written English, we state our topic and we elaborate on our statement by adding supporting g details, such as facts, examples, descriptions, illustrations, reasons, cause, affects, comparisons, and contrasts.

Additionally, multiple texts are used across all subject areas to convey "multiple viewpoints in multiple formats (e.g., letters, essays, reports, advertisements, lectures), through various venues (e.g., newspapers, television, postcards, websites, books, magazines)..." (Shanahan, 2008). Shanahan (2008) further postulates that adolescence need instruction to use effective strategies in writing about the same topic in multiple ways and for multiple purposes. Students need to learn to keep the audience in mind and the kind of writing they are engaged in. They can use the techniques mentioned below to help them identify this beforehand.

Organizing thoughts in writing is a process in itself. A number of strategies can be used to teach students these skills. They allow the students to make choices with the purpose of the task in mind. Following are some techniques that would help students with their organization skills.

1. Outlines

There are two basic types of outlines:

- An outline the writer makes before writing the text;
- An outline the writer makes of what he has already written.

An outline that is developed before writing the text should be brief and made after extensive discussion, list-making, brainstorming, and other prewriting activities. It helps to guide the writer in developing the text. Similarly, an outline that is made after the first draft is written helps the writer analyze his/her work and see what needs to be done to make the text more clearly to the reader. A technique to teach this skill would be to give the students a reading passage and ask them either to discuss and make their own outline of what has been written or to complete the skeleton of a given outline.

2. Analysis

Outlining is one way to help students examine a text closely. Additionally, students should also analyze a reading passage and ask questions about a piece of writing regarding not only what the writer has written but also how he/she has written it. Some techniques to teach this skill are: (a) Students are given short paragraphs and asked to read one sentence of each. Then they are asked to discuss in pairs or in groups which one sentence best express the paragraph it belongs to and why. (b) Give or read students a paragraph without its topic sentence or the concluding sentence. Then ask the students to choose from the choices provided and also giving reasons for their choice. If the students are advanced, then they could discuss the passage and write their own sentences.

3. Models

Model paragraphs or texts should not be used for students to imitate and use mechanically but they should be used as a resource for the writer. For example, the students might read a passage comparing two bicycles and then they write their own composition comparing two cars, following the organizational and structural pattern of the model as closely as possible. Instead of following the model, it should be used as a resource to help students deal with the problem that emerges in the process of their own writing. For example, if the student is not sure how to best organize an argument, then the model can be used to analyze, or manipulate and shed a light on what path to take.

Skill 10.4 Selecting purposeful writing activities that are appropriate to a range of ages and proficiency levels (e.g., friendly letters, book reports, research papers)

To keep students engaged in a writing task, it is important for the writer to be interested in the task. Therefore, these tasks need a purpose to it than just *language practice*. Personal topics (such as autobiography, hobbies, preferences, problems) allow students to convey real information. However, when topics move away from personal narratives, it is helpful to specify the communicative purpose of the topic. A topic like, "A vacation on a cruise ship is a wonderful experience" can be changed to "Write an advertisement for a cruise ship and to convince people to take a cruise rather than fly to new place". Therefore, while selecting a topic, it is necessary to consider how to make it meaningful for both the reader and the writer This way the writer will put more effort and interest into his/her writing in order to communicate real meaning.

For beginning level students, the first steps in teaching wiring skills in an ESL classroom cater around the mechanics of the skill. This means letter recognition, letter discrimination, word recognition, basic rules of spelling, punctuation and capitalization, including recognition of whole sentences and paragraphs. Recognition and writing drills are the initial steps that help in the development of effective writing skills.

Three main types of recognition tasks are usually used at the early stages of learning:

1. *Matching tasks:* These are effective recognition tasks that are mostly in the form of games, puzzles, etc.
2. *Writing tasks:* At this early stage of writing, it is important to get learners accustomed to correct capitalization in English and to basic punctuation rules.
3. *Meaningful sound spelling correspondence practice:* Students write meaningful sentences (accompanied by pictures) which show sound-spelling correspondences. They constitute correct capitalization and punctuation rules as well as have words that students have recently learned. These sentences may not be as interesting but fulfills its purpose. Eventually, this language knowledge works as the basis for developing more meaningful and interesting texts.

The next step focuses on the basic process-oriented tasks which incorporates some language at the morphological and discourse level. Therefore, these activities will focus on both accuracy and content of the message. It caters to a wide range of proficiency levels, depending on the specifications of the task.

These include:

1. *Practical writing tasks:* These wiring tasks have a predictable format. This makes them suitable for writing activities that focus primarily on spelling and morphology. These include various types of lists, notes, short messages, simple instructions, etc. It caters to beginning and intermediate level students.

2. *Emotive writing tasks:* These are concerned with personal writing which include letters to friends and narratives describing personal experiences, as well as personal journals and diaries. These writing activates are suitable for intermediate and advanced learners but can also be used at the beginning level in a limited manner. For example, letters can be limited to the level of structural and vocabulary knowledge of the students as they increase in their proficiency level. Therefore, it is necessary to provide students with specifications of the tasks in order for them to respond according to their proficiency levels.

3. *School-oriented tasks*: The function of writing in school is the most important aspect of students' writing. A lot of individual learning takes place when students are writing assignments, summaries, answers to questions, book reports, research papers, or a variety of essay-type passages. The teacher could be the audience of these writing tasks, but eventually the students should be engaged in activities that convey information to multiple audiences across multiple genres (Shanahan, 2008). At an early stage of ESL learning, the assignments should be short and limited. Answers might be single phrases or sentences, and summaries could be just listing of main ideas. However, at a higher proficiency level, the activities could require more complex structure and organization skills catering to multiple audiences and also skills involving writing across different genres (e.g., research papers, scientific journals and magazines, newspaper article, etc).

Appropriate task selection involves a variety of factors, but it is also important to use a variety of writing tasks at all levels of student learning. Writing is a vital communication skill, but it also enables the learner to plan and think about this process. Therefore, the learner focuses on both linguistic accuracy and content organization.

Skill 10.5 Applying instructional strategies that address conventions of English grammar, usage, and mechanics.

There has been a lot of discussion regarding the role of grammar in the teaching of writing. Research has shown grammar to be an aid for language users to effectively communicate their ideas and to make meaning clear and precise. Therefore, the purpose of the teacher is not to teach grammar for error correction but to use it to address specific needs of the students and to develop appropriate instructional materials for learners at all stages of the writing process. It is important to include grammar-oriented activities not only to help students edit errors in their writing but also to help them understand how grammar contributes to meaning (Frodesen, 1991). Following are the specific strategies and techniques to help achieve this goal.

1. *Text Analysis*
   Text analysis can provide ESL students to see how particular grammatical features are used to write a particular kind of text in order to communicate the writer's purpose. It also helps writer's understand and use appropriate grammatical oppositions such as definite and indefinite articles, restrictive and nonrestrictive clauses, and present perfect and past or present tense verb forms. However, these exercises should usually be kept short because the real focus of a writing class is to improve the writing skills of the ESL students. The goal should be to identify and explain the functions of grammatical structures in discourse contexts.

2. *Guided Writing Practice*
   The focus of guided writing is on a particular grammatical structure in order to address the grammar problems of learners prevalent in their writing. This helps build confidence in the ESL learners to use particular grammatical structures that they find difficult and to develop syntactic complexity in their writing. However, guided writing activates are now used as not simply grammar practice but as components of prewriting, revising, or editing stages of the writing process. Some examples are:

   - Dictation: It helps students diagnose and correct their errors in grammar.
   - Text Elicitation: The teacher specifies both a topic and grammatical construction/constructions to be used.
   - Text conversion: Students are given paragraphs or short texts to rewrite, changing some feature of the grammatical structure, for example present tense to past tense. These activities should be as relevant as possible to actual writing.
   - Text completion: Two common types of these activities are the cloze passage and the gapped text.

3. *Editing*
   The focus of these activities is to develop students' abilities to detect and correct errors so they would become effective editors of their writing.

   - Error Detection/ Correction Exercises These activities are designed to help students identify and correct the kinds of errors frequently made in their writing, and help intermediate and advanced writers develop systematic strategies for writing. Therefore, whenever possible and appropriate, students' actual text should be used for this task.
   - Read-Aloud Techniques: During this activity, students read their paper aloud and listen to errors and correct them as they proceed. Students could also work in pairs and help each other make the corrections.

4. *Teacher Correction and Feedback on Errors:*
   Teachers should help students identify and correct frequent error pattern and devise ways for them to observe improvement in their work over a short period of time. Another method suggested by Celce-Murcia Hilles (1988) is the *blue sheet*. In this strategy, the teacher attaches a blue sheet with each student's paragraph or essay on which two errors are listed that need immediate attention. This is followed by guided practice of these errors in the classroom. Additionally, teacher-student conferences can provide more individualized help with grammar problems in writing. It could be done in small groups as well. This helps teacher take up the role of a collaborator and help students set goals for improvement and suggest effective correction strategies.

Skill 10.6 Selecting or creating appropriate assessments for given testing purposes and situations.

It is argued that the *direct testing of writing* is most effective which requires the students to *write*. According to Hughes (1989), there are three general problems concerning testing writing:

1. We have to set writing tasks that are properly representative of the population of tasks that we should expect the students to be able to perform.
2. The tasks should elicit samples of writing which truly represent the student's ability.
3. It is essential that the samples of writing can and will be scored reliably.

Specifying all appropriate tasks and selecting a sample
When preparing the test, it is essential that the tasks represent what we expect the students to be able to perform on the test. This should be identified before we start creating the test.

Set as many tasks as possible
If we want to create a valid test, than it should require the students to produce writings in a variety of writing tasks. The total score of this type of test would be fair estimate of the students' ability.

Tests only writing ability
Tests should not set tasks that evaluate students' intelligence, general knowledge, or good support for their opinions. Additionally, we should not make the instructions difficult or long for the students to have problem in comprehending it.

Well-defined tasks
When responding to a task, students' should know what is required of them and should not astray from the topic. However, teachers should be careful not to provide too much information in the instruction which could help students perform the task. For example, complete sentences should be avoided which could be used as it is in the composition.

Selecting task that could be scored reliably
The following could help maintain the reliability of a writing test:

- Set as many tasks as possible
- Restrict students
- Give no choice on tasks
- Ensure long enough samples

Reliable scoring of writing samples

1) **Holistic scoring**: In this type of scoring, a single score is given to the writing piece on the basis of an overall impression of it. This helps to score quickly and therefore one piece of writing can be scored more than once to ensure reliability. However, this scoring system should be appropriate to the level of the candidates and the purpose of the test.

2) **Analytic methods of scoring**: This method of scoring requires a separate score for a number of subskills. This varies according to the purpose of the test and may include grammar, vocabulary, mechanics, fluency (style of communication), and form (organization). This kind of scoring helps assess and diagnose all subskills as well as make the test reliable because it is given a number of scores (one for each subskill). However, the scoring takes longer and the division into subskills might divert the assessment on the overall effort of the writing.

The choice of the type of scoring depends on the purpose of the test, but it is important that the scorers should be trained in using these scales. Additionally, each writing sample of the student should be scored independently by two or more scorers and should be recorded on separate sheets. A third member of the test team should search for any discrepancies in the scores given to the same piece of writing.

In addition to standard tests, informal assessment is an effective way to test students' progress regularly. This helps teachers focus on students' problem areas, adapt instruction, and to ensure learning. Typical classroom activities are used to measure progress with respect to curricular goals and objectives. There are two commonly used informal methods: performance-based assessment and portfolio assessment

Performance-Based Activities:
This type of assessment is based on the tasks and activities done in the classroom. Some of the activities are oral reports, presentations, demonstrations, and written assignments. Both process (e.g. several drafts of a writing sample as well as product (e.g. research paper) can become a part of this assessment. This helps to monitor the student's growth over a period of time and get the real sense of their improvement. Scoring rubrics and observation checklist can be utilized to evaluate the students' ability and progress. However, it is important to have clear and fair evaluation criteria from the beginning.

Portfolio Assessments
Portfolio assessment helps teachers maintain a record of their students' work for the entire school year. This makes it possible for both the teachers and the students to view students' progress throughout the year. Portfolio includes information, sample work, and evaluations that serve as students' progress records.

Competency 11   **UNDERSTAND THE SELECTION, ADAPTATION, AND USE OF MATERIALS FOR VARIOUS INSTRUCTIONAL PURPOSES IN THE ESOL CLASSROOM**

Skill 11.1   **Defining appropriate criteria for evaluating instructional materials**

In considering suitable learning materials for the classroom, the teacher must have a thorough understanding of the state-mandated competency-based curriculum. According to state requirements, certain objectives must be met in each subject taught at every designated level of instruction. It is necessary that the teacher become well acquainted with the curriculum for which he or she is assigned. The teacher must also be aware that it is unlawful to require students to study from textbooks or materials other than those approved by the State Department of Education.

Keeping in mind the state requirements concerning the objectives and materials, the teacher must determine the abilities of the incoming students assigned to his or her class or supervision. It is essential to be aware of their entry behavior—that is, their current level of achievement in the relevant areas. The next step is to take a broad overview of students who are expected to learn before they are passed on to the next grade or level of instruction. Finally, the teacher must design a course of study that will enable students to reach the necessary level of achievement, as displayed in their final assessments, or exit behaviors. Textbooks and learning materials must be chosen to fit into this context.

Once students' abilities are determined, the teacher will select the learning materials for the class. In choosing materials, teachers should also keep in mind that not only do students learn at different rates, but they bring a variety of cognitive styles to the learning process. Prior experiences influence the individual's cognitive style, or method of accepting, processing, and retaining information.

Most teachers chose to use textbooks and other teaching materials, which are suitable to the age and developmental level of specific student populations. They should also keep in mind the diverse background of the students and try to incorporate the different cultures in their teaching materials. Additionally, in the ESL classroom, it is recommended to use authentic texts as much as possible and to adapt them if necessary according to the proficiency level of the students ($I = 1$). Similarly, the needs of the students should also be addressed. In K-12 setting, students are expected have the proficient enough in academic English (CALP) to succeed in school. Therefore, the focus of the materials (especially for secondary level students, should be to teach them strategies that would help them achieve the skills necessary for this purpose.

Aside from textbooks, a wide variety of materials are available to today's teachers. Computers are now commonplace, and some schools can now afford DVDs to bring alive the content of a reference book in text, motion, and sound. Videocassettes (VCR's) are common and permit the use of home-produced or commercially produced tapes. Textbook publishers often provide films, recordings, and software to accompany the text, as well as flow charts, graphics, and colorful posters to help students visualize what is being taught. Teachers can usually scan the educational publishers' brochures that arrive at their principal's or department head's office on a frequent basis. Another way to stay current in the field is by attending workshops or conferences. Teachers will be enthusiastically welcomed on those occasions when educational publishers are asked to display their latest productions and revised editions of materials.

Skill 11.2   Selecting appropriate materials for given instructional purposes (e.g., making content accessible)

One of the great challenges of middle school and high school teachers is to make content accessible to students with limited proficiency in English. Some content materials can be difficult for ESL students and teachers need to implement ways to make content accessible for these students. For this purpose, teachers should encourage their students to use **graphic organizers** such as, web, Venn diagrams, and charts to help them better comprehend these texts. These visual tools help ELLs visualize and organize information and promote active learning. Not only does it encourage creativity and high-order thinking skills, but also help students summarize and interpret texts.

In order to make content accessible, teachers need to determine the appropriate level of language to use for instruction for the given ELL population. Additionally, teachers should (Loughlin & Haynes, 1999):

- Simplify the language of instruction, not the content being taught.
- Eliminate nonessential information and present materials in a clear, concise, and comprehensible manner.
- Teach the material in multiple ways, through oral, visual, auditory, and kinesthetic learning modalities.
- Preteach content area vocabulary and concepts, using realia, picture files, and hands-on activities.
- Checking for comprehension during instruction and structuring opportunities for students to use English.
- Use materials (or create them) that simplify the language of abstract concepts by retelling content information in easier English. Depending on the proficiency level of the students, teachers should use simple sentence structure and high frequency verbs.
- Select materials that help students build connections and associations in order to access background knowledge or previously taught information. This can be accomplished through teacher prepared outlines and study guides.

- Present students with written as well as aural messages. Outline what you are saying on the chalkboard.
- Allowing students' use of native language for English language and concept development.
- Model think-alouds to increase student comprehension. *Think-alouds* are oral demonstration of the teacher's own cognitive processes or the strategies they use to comprehend the text. Students then try to incorporate these strategies to help them in the learning process. Teachers explicitly teach these strategies until the learners are able to use them independently.

Skill 11.3   Demonstrating knowledge of the use of content-area test, children and adolescent literature, and multicultural literature in the ESOL classroom

Some English language learners (ELLs) know very little English, but have a rich content background from their primary language. Other ELLs may have acquired intermediate or advanced English skills, but still have gaps in their content knowledge. In order for ELLs to become successful overall students, they need to learn both English and grade-level content. English language teachers teach **content area subjects** in the classroom, but at times they also need to teach them from the original text without making it simple for their students. These teachers can adopt certain strategies that would give additional support to the ELLs in their learning of content-are subjects such as, moths, science, literature, etc. Some of the strategies are as follows:

- *Introducing a text before reading*: Pre-reading activities may be designed to motivate student interest, activate prior knowledge, or pre-teach potentially difficult concepts and vocabulary. This is also a great opportunity to introduce comprehension components such as cause and effect, compare and contrast, personification, main idea, sequencing, and others. Some pre-reading activities could be showing a film on a related topic, conducting an experiment, going on a field trip, etc.
- *Cooperative learning strategies:* Cooperative learning is particularly beneficial for any student learning a second language. Cooperative Learning activities promote peer interaction, which helps the development of language and the learning of concepts and content. It is important to assign ELLs to different teams so that they can benefit from English language role models. ELLs learn to express themselves with greater confidence when working in small teams. In addition to 'picking up' vocabulary, ELLs benefit from observing how their peers learn and solve problems. There are a number of such group activities that help students gain content as well as language at the same time. An example is *team jigsaw* in which each student in a team is assigned one fourth of a page to read from any text (for example, a social studies text), or one fourth of a topic to investigate or memorize. Each student completes his or her assignment and then teaches the others or helps to put together a team product by contributing a piece of the puzzle.

- *Explicit teaching of reading comprehension skills:* English language learners (ELLs) often have problems mastering science, math, or social studies concepts because they cannot comprehend the textbooks for these subjects. Teaching comprehension strategies help students apply these skills to all subject areas. These skills include: summarizing, sequencing, Inferencing, comparing and contrasting, drawing conclusions, self-questioning, problem solving, relating background knowledge, and distinguishing between fact and opinion.

Another important cooperative group strategy for **teaching literature** could be the introduction of *literacy circle* in the classroom. Literature circles are group meetings in which students get together to read, recollect, reflect, and analyze the assigned reading/book just like a book club. Teachers may use this activity to promote comprehension, as well as vocabulary skills. When ELLs are included in literature circles they have the opportunity to interact with peers and can also invite English proficient students as they model appropriate language skills.

Working in groups provides ELLs with an opportunity to reflect and relate elements from the reading back to their personal experiences. ELLs may also benefit from interactive oral discussions, which allow them to gain a deeper level of understanding about the subject. Once second language learners have had an opportunity to listen to their peers discuss the book, they can begin to build knowledge and develop higher order thinking skills. Another method of introducing literature circles is to require students to work in centers. These literature circles can also be "active learning centers." Here students are allowed to discuss the assigned book using pictures, charts, and visual representations which benefits ELLs' comprehension of the book. Examples of these centers are:

1. *Vocabulary Center — "Definition Detectives"* Students are responsible for finding unfamiliar words and describing their meaning, which they later share with the class. Students may choose to either create a presentation or a poster with the definitions they have found.

2. *Basic Story Elements Center — "Advertising Agents"* Students in this group need to find the main idea, characters, and story line to create a movie poster advertisement for the story.

3. *Summarizing Center — "Cartoon Creators"* Students are responsible for summarizing the main parts of the story. They need to write a summarizing sentence for each page or chapter and need to create cartoon frames for each of their sentences.

4. *Research Center — "Research Wranglers"* Students in this group are responsible for looking up information related to the book on the Internet or the school library, which they later present to the classroom in a poster form.

Multicultural literature can be used as an effective tool to teach literacy skills in an English language classroom. It helps to acknowledge the diversity of cultures in the classroom, where students feel proud of their own culture as well as learn about other cultures as well. Multicultural literature not only celebrates different cultures, but also helps students relate to the text at hand. Students are able to activate their background knowledge thus improving their comprehension of the text at hand.

Skill 11.4   Creating and adapting materials to meet the needs, interests, and proficiency levels of students

The effective teacher will seek to connect all students to the subject matter using multiple techniques. With the goal being that each student, through their own abilities, will relate to one or more techniques and excel in the learning process. While all students need to have exposure to the same curriculum, not all students need to have the curriculum taught in the same way. Differentiation is the term used to describe the variations of curriculum and instruction that can be provided to an entire class of students.

The following are three primary ways to differentiate:

- Content—The specifics of what is learned. This does not mean that whole units or concepts should be modified. However, within certain topics, specifics can be modified.
- Process—The route to learning the content. This means that not everyone has to learn the content in exactly the same method.
- Product—The result of the learning. Usually, a product is the end result or assessment of learning. For example, not all students are going to demonstrate complete learning on a quiz; likewise, not all students will demonstrate complete learning on a written paper.

The following are two keys to successful differentiation:

- Knowing what is essential in the curriculum. Although certain things can be modified, other things must remain in-tact in a specific order. Disrupting central components of a curriculum can actually damage a student's ability to learn something successfully.
- Knowing the needs of the students. While this can take quite some time to figure out, it is very important that teachers pay attention to the interests, tendencies, and abilities of their students so that they understand how each of their students will best learn.

Many students will need certain concepts explained in greater depth; others may pick up on concepts rather quickly. For this reason, teachers will want to adapt the curriculum in a way that allows students with the opportunity to learn at their own pace, while also keeping the class together as a community. While this can be difficult, the more creative a teacher is with the ways in which students can demonstrate mastery, the more fun the experience will be for students and teachers. Furthermore, teachers will reach students more successfully as they will tailor lesson plans, activities, groupings, and other elements of curriculum to each student's need.

Studies have shown students learn best when what is taught in lecture and textbook reading is presented more than once in a variety of formats. In some instances, students themselves may be asked to reinforce what they have learned by completing some original production—for example, by drawing pictures to explain action verb, by writing a monologue or dialogue to express reading comprehension, by devising a board game to learn some grammatical concepts, or by acting out (and perhaps filming) episodes from a classroom reading selection. Students usually enjoy having their work displayed or presented to an audience of peers. Thus, their productions may supplement and personalize the learning experiences that the teacher has planned for them.

The effective teacher takes care to select appropriate activities and classroom situations in which learning is optimized. The classroom teacher should manipulate instructional activities and classroom conditions in a manner that enhances group and individual learning opportunities. For example, the classroom teacher can organize group learning activities in which students are placed in a situation in which cooperation, sharing ideas, and discussion occurs. Cooperative learning activities can assist students in learning to collaborate and share personal and cultural ideas and values in a classroom learning environment.

(For more detail on this topic, see Skill 11.2)

Skill 11.5   Recognizing ways to integrate technologies in the classroom for given instructional purposes.

The tools teachers have available to them to present information to students are always growing. Where just ten years ago, teachers needed to only know how to use word processing programs, grading programs, and overhead projectors, today, electronic slideshows (most people think of Power Point) are becoming the new "norm," and other methods of information distribution are expected by principals, parents, and students alike.

Educational technology as a learning tool can increase learning opportunities for English language students. Developing effective and adequate strategies is crucial to integrate technology in multiple ways in the ESL classroom. Competent use of computers prevents ELLs from "academic and social marginalization" (Murray & Kouritzin, 1997, p.187). It allows them to have the most control over the direction of their learning by controlling their time, speed of learning, autonomy, choice of topics or even their own identity (Hoven, 1992). Technology gives English Language learners prompt feedback, individualizes their learning, and tailors the instructional sequence. It can meet specific student needs, increase their autonomy, allow for more responsibility, promote equal opportunities in an early nonsexist environment, encourage student cooperation with peers, and encourage them to make decisions (Burgess & Trinidad, 1997).

Tools such as e-mail, databases, spreadsheets, or word processors can help enhance ELLs' English skills—and, if necessary, build on their native language skills through the availability of online dictionaries or spellcheckers (Johns & Tórrez, 2001). Technology has evolved from its support function to play a role in initiating learning processes. It can provide a flexible learning environment where students can really explore and be engaged. Hypermedia, for example, individually addresses levels of fluency, content knowledge, student motivation, and interest, allowing inclusion of English language students, who can thus monitor their comprehension, language production, and behavior (Bermudez & Palumbo, 1994).

Technology integration defined by Reilly (2002) is curriculum development. It is one way to move teaching from teacher- to learner-centered. To allow for greater success rates for ELLs, teachers need to integrate technology to advance student learning because technology activities, such as using the Internet or working as a team on a project, provide students with opportunities in order to enhance and extend the regular learning to higher levels of cognitive involvement The effect of engaging English language students through technology can be multilayered. When technology is used as part of a model that involves students in complex authentic tasks, the results can be student-centered cooperative learning, increased teacher-student and peer interaction, and more positive attitudes toward learning, allowing greater interaction and sense of responsibility as a team.

Internet and software can enrich the learning process, where students can look up art work and other content area information. These activities can accelerate content learning by addressing relevant information and are not solely dependent on learning English. Through experiences such as these, ELLs have the opportunities to participate in an engaged learning environment and learn at higher levels. With technology, these students can control and self-direct their learning and get immediate feedback. They no longer depend on direct teacher instruction, which often limits the student to passive listening and watching the teacher. While the direct teacher control is evidently lower in technology-based classrooms (e.g., a computer lab), the instruction is ever more demanding on the teacher. The teacher becomes a facilitator, rather than a "deliverer or transmitter of knowledge" (Padrón & Waxman, 1996, p. 348). Teachers scaffold their students' learning experiences to build high-quality instruction.

The following are some activities using technology that are intended to support learner knowledge construction:

1. Online collaboration with classrooms around the world.

2. Education applications of the Web such as e-mail exchanges, online bulletin board, and information searching.

3. The use of multimedia to create projects (Hartley & Bendixen, 2001).

When students are engaged in activities like these, they are constructing their own knowledge, with the teacher as the facilitator of the process.

Incorporating technology effectively into a fully content- and skill-based curriculum requires a good understanding of lesson objectives and how those objectives can be met with the technology. While teachers should definitely consider technological integration as an important aspect of their work in any subject and at any grade level, teachers should not include technology simply for the sake of technology. The best approach, considering all subjects can in certain ways be enhanced with technology, is for the teacher to consider a variety of lessons and units and decide which focus areas can be enhanced with technological tools.

Finally, it is important to remember that as with all other learning, technological learning must be developmentally-appropriate. First, realize that while very young students can perform various functions on the computer, by virtue of development level, the time required for a particular activity may be greatly increased. Also, various technological tools are simply too advanced, too fast, and too complex for very young students. It may be best to introduce basic elements of technology in the earlier grades.

Competency 12   UNDERSTAND APPROACHES TO FACILITATING CONTENT-AREA LEARNING FOR ENGLISH LANGUAGE LEARNERS

Skill 12.1   Demonstrating knowledge of techniques for using students' linguistic and cultural diversity to enhance content-area learning

It is important to implement powerful instructional strategies that actively engage students from linguistically and culturally diverse backgrounds instead of allowing them to be passive participants or observers. Chamot and O'Malley (1994) stated that teachers need to be aware of their students' approaches to learning and how to expand the students' repertoire of learning strategies. According to Arreaga-Mayer ((1998), language sensitive content instruction based on effective and efficient learning strategies must (a) be effective for culturally and linguistically homogenous learning groups; (b) lead to high levels of student and student-student active engagement in learning; (c) foster higher-order cognitive processes; (d) enable students to encourage in extended discourse in English; (e) be feasible to implement on a small-group or class wide basis; (f) be socially acceptable to the teachers, students, and parents; and (g) be responsive to cultural and personal diversity.

In addition to this, Arreaga-Mayer ((1998) puts forward constructs for effective instruction to linguistically and culturally diverse students:

1. *Challenge*:
    - Implicit (cognitive challenge, use of higher-order questions)
    - Explicit (high but reasonable expectations)
2. *Involvement:*
    - Active involvement of all students
3. *Success*
    - Reasonable activities that students can complete successfully.
4. *Scaffolding/cognitive strategies*
    - Visual organizers, adequate background information, and support provided by teachers to students by thinking-aloud, building on and clarifying their input
5. *Mediation/feedback*
    - Strategies provided to students
    - Frequency and comprehensibility stressed
6. *Collaborative/cooperative learning*
7. *Techniques for second language acquisition/sheltered English*
    - Extended discourse fostered
    - Use of consistent language
    - Incorporation of student's language
8. *Respect for cultural diversity*
    - Respect and knowledge of cultural diversity

Additionally, **peer-mediated instruction** is affective in promoting higher levels of language and academic learning and social interaction. Research has shown that cooperative peer-mediated instruction contributes more to content mastery than do whole-class instruction, workbook activities, and question-answer sessions. This method gives ELLs opportunities to actively practice a concept, the amount of discourse produced, and degree of negotiation of meaning, the amount of comprehensible linguistic input for the learners. The essential components of peer-mediated learning strategies are: (a) cooperative incentives, (b) group rewards, (c) individual accountability, and (d) task structures.

In this method, students of varied academic abilities and language proficiency levels work together in pairs and small groups toward a common goal. In these groups, the success of one student depends on the help of the others. In peer-mediated instruction the learning task assigned to groups varies, but the format of learning always includes interaction and independence among the students.

Similarly, **peer tutoring** is a method developed to improve the acquisition and retention of basic academic skills. In this method, students are either paired randomly or matched be ability or language proficiency to partners each week. Student's roles are switched during the daily tutoring session, allowing each child to be both the tutor/teacher and the tutee/student. Students are trained in the procedures necessary to act as tutors and tutees. The four basic components of this method are:

- Weekly competing teams (culturally, linguistically, and ability-wise heterogeneous grouping)
- Highly structured teaching procedure (content material, teams, pairing, error correction, system of rewards)
- Daily, contingent, individual tutee point earning and public postings of individual and team scores.
- Direct practice of functional academic and language skills to mastery

Skill 12.2   Identifying linguistic characteristics and applying methods for developing students' cognitive- academic language proficiency in content areas

Academic English refers to the language used by the educated and is needed function at the university level and beyond. In order to achieve socioeconomic success, it si important for students to perform at an appropriate academic level. **Cognitive Academic Language Proficiency (CALP)** refers to the language skills required for academic achievement and are usually more difficult to acquire than BICS. Cummins (1993-2003) states that it takes from five to seven years for students to acquire CALP after initial exposure to a second language.

The linguistic aspect of Cognitive Academic Language (CALP) include the following areas: phonological, lexical, grammatical, sociolinguistics, and discourse (Uribe, 2008).

1. The phonological component
    *   Knowledge of everyday English sounds and the ways sounds are combined, stress and intonation, graphemes, and spelling. For example, ship versus sheep /I/ - /i/, sheet versus cheat /sh/ - /ch/
    *   Knowledge of the phonological features (including spelling: *research, although*) of academic English, including stress, intonation, and sound patterns. For example, demography, demographic, cadence, generic, casualty, and celerity.
2. The lexical component:

*   Knowledge of the forms and meanings of words occurring in everyday situations; *knowledge* of the ways words are formed with prefixes, roots, suffixes, the parts of the speech of words, and the grammatical constraints governing words   For example, find out, look for.
*   Knowledge of the forms and meanings of words that are used across academic disciplines (*assert, hypothesis*) as well as in everyday settings; Knowledge of the ways academic words are formed with prefixes, roots, and suffixes, the parts of speech of academic words, and the grammatical constraints governing academic words. For example, investigate, research, seek.

3. The grammatical component:

*   Knowledge of morphemes entailing semantic, syntactic, relational, phonological, and distributional properties; knowledge of syntax; *knowledge* of simple rules of punctuation. For example, he was runned by a car, knifes, mines, if I was you.
*   Knowledge that enables EL´s to make sense out of and use the grammatical features (morphological and syntactic) associated with argumentative composition, procedural description, analysis, definition, procedural description, and analysis; Knowledge of the grammatical co-occurrence restrictions governing words; Knowledge of grammatical metaphor; Knowledge of more complex rules of punctuation. For example, he was run by a car, knives, mine, if I were you.

4. The sociolinguistic component:

*   Knowledge that enables EL´s to understand the extent to which sentences are produced and understood appropriately; *knowledge* of frequently occurring functions and genres. For example, what´s up? (to a professor).
*   Knowledge of an increased number of language functions. The functions include the general ones of ordinary English such as apologizing, complaining, and making requests as well as ones that are common to all academic fields; knowledge of an increased number of genres, including expository and argumentative text. For example, how are you doing, sir?

5. The discourse component:

- Knowledge of the basic discourse devices used, for instance, to introduce topics and keep the talk going and for beginning and ending informal types of writing, such letters and lists / For example, but, it was.
- Knowledge of the discourse features used in specific academic genres including such devices as transitions and other organizational signals that, in reading, aid in gaining perspective on what is read, in seeing relationships, and in following logical lines of thought; in writing, these discourse features help EL´s develop their theses and provide smooth
transitions between ideas. For example, nevertheless, once upon a time.

Academic tasks tend to increase in their cognitive demands as students progress in their schooling, but the context becomes increasingly reduced. ELLs who have not developed CALP need additional teacher support to achieve success. Contextual support in the form of realia, demonstrations, pictures, graphs, etc. provide the ELL with scaffolding and reduce the language difficulty level of the task. Both content and ESOL teachers should incorporate teaching academic skills in their lessons. The following are essential elements to include in teaching academic English:

1. Integrate listening, speaking, reading, and writing skills in all lessons for all proficiencies.
2. Teaching the components and processes of reading and writing.
3. Focusing on vocabulary development.
4. Building and activating prior knowledge.
5. Teaching language through content and themes.
6. Using native language strategically.
7. Pairing technology with instruction.
8. Motivating ELLs with choice.

(See also Skill 12.1)

Skill 12.3   Demonstrate the ability to devise and implement thematic units that integrate content and language objectives and help English language learners acquire content-area knowledge and skills

A number of program models have been developed to meet the needs of language minority students involving the integration of language and content instruction. In this approach, the second or foreign language is used as the medium of instruction for mathematics, science, social studies, and other academic subjects; it is the vehicle used for teaching and acquiring subject specific knowledge. The focus of the second language classroom should be on something meaningful, such as academic content, and that modification of the target language facilitates language acquisition and makes academic content accessible to second language learners.

Integrated language and content instruction offers a means by which English as a second language (ESL) students can continue their academic or cognitive development while they are also acquiring academic language proficiency. In **theme-based programs**, a language curriculum is developed around selected topics drawn from one content area (e.g., marketing) or from across the curriculum (e.g., pollution and the environment). The theme could be a week or two long and would focus on language taught in a meaningful way. The goal is to assist learners in developing general academic language skills through interesting and relevant content. There are a variety of strategies to teach the integrated approach to language teaching of which the four most important are (Crandall, 1994):

1. *Cooperative learning:* In this method, students of different linguistic and educational backgrounds and different skill levels work together on a common task for a common goal to complete a task pertaining to the content being taught in the classroom. The focus is also on an implicit or explicit language feature that the students acquire through negotiation of meaning.
2. *Task-based or experiential learning:* Appropriate contexts are provided for developing thinking and study skills as well as language and academic concepts for students of different levels of language proficiency. Students learn by carrying out specific tasks or projects that they complete with a focus on the content, but learning language and academic skills as well.
3. *Whole language approach:* The philosophy of whole language is based on the concept that students need to experience language as an integrated whole. It focuses on the need for an integrated approach to language instruction within a context that is meaningful to students (Goodman, 1986). The approach is consistent with integrated language and content instruction as both emphasize meaningful engagement and authentic language use, and both link oral and written language development (Blanton, 1992). Whole language strategies that have been implemented in content-centered language classes include dialogue journals, reading response journals, learning logs, process-based writing, and language experience stories (Crandall, 1992).
4. *Graphic organizers*: These provide a "means for organizing and presenting information so that it can be understood, remembered, and applied" (Crandall, 1992). Graphs, realia, tables, maps, flow charts, timelines, and Venn diagrams are used to help students place information in a comprehensible context. They enable students to organize information obtained from written or oral texts, develop reading strategies, increase retention, activate schema as a pre-reading or pre-listening activity, and organize ideas during the prewriting stage (Crandall, 1992).

Skill 12.4   Utilizing strategies for selecting and adapting content-area curricula to meet the cognitive and linguistic needs of English language learners

Content-based instruction (CBI) or "Sheltered Instruction" integrates L2 acquisition and the basic content areas of math, science, social studies, literature, etc. The most current research continues to find validity in the following:

- *Learners do not learn L2 through singular instruction in the language's rules; they learn from meaningful interaction in the language.*
- *Learners will gain proficiency in a language, only if they receive adequate input, i.e., speaking and listening start to make sense to a learner when they can build upon previous knowledge as well as understand context and cues.*
- *Although conversational fluency in L2 is a goal, speaking is not sufficient to develop the academic cognitive skills needed to learn the basic content areas.*

The goal in every classroom is for Limited English Proficiency (LEP) students to learn the basic content areas (math, science, social studies, etc.) To accomplish this goal, LEP students must learn an "academic language" which takes from five to seven years (Cummins, 1993-2003), because LEP students typically encounter issues with vocabulary when being instructed in the content areas.

The following are strategies for CBI or "Sheltered Instructional Delivery":

When speaking, instructors should:
- Speak slower, but naturally, taking care to enunciate without raising the volume
- Use short sentences when explaining a concept or instructions
- Use instructional strategies like repeating or rephrasing
- Write new vocabulary, expressions, or idioms on the board for further reinforcement

When solving word problems in math, the instructors should first:
- Work through a word problem with the student step-by-step
- Demonstrate various strategies for problem-solving

When providing contextualization, the instructor should:
- Use facial expressions and gestures
- Use realia (cultural objects)
- Use visual cues, such as pictures, blackboard sketches, DVDs, videos, slides, transparencies, etc.
- Use graphic organizers

When giving directions, the instructor should:
- Simplify complicated tasks by giving specific instructions such as, "Open to page 107. Read the story. Once you have finished, wait for the class to finish reading."
- Periodically check for comprehension during the lesson.
- The instructor should provide opportunities for learner interactions.
- Cooperative learning groups are essential for LEP learners with varying levels of proficiency; "heterogeneous" groupings help to improve academic performance, especially if LEP students have the opportunity to clarify concepts and ask questions in their primary language.

When checking for understanding, the instructor should:
- Ask the learners to clarify the first, second, and continuing steps of a process.
- Ask a "who," "what," "when," "where," or "whose" question.
- Ask silly questions.
- Ask for clarification from the learner.

When correcting an error, the instructor should:
- NEVER embarrass or humiliate a LEP learner.
- Avoid corrections when possible and simply accept the ELL's efforts at language attempts. Model the language correctly without comments.
- Keep error correction to a minimum at first.
- Emphasize that making mistakes and being corrected is a basic tenet of any learning process but especially when learning a language.
- Focus on what a learner is trying to communicate rather than on how correct the communication is.
- When the error interferes with understanding, restate the question or sentence correctly.
-

Included with the preceding strategies, are the following reminders: always announce and write down the objectives for a particular unit, use handwriting that is readable, develop consistency through daily routines, list step-by-step instructions, and use blended instructional approaches, whenever possible.

Skill 12.5   Applying knowledge of instructional strategies that help students build on their prior knowledge and experience

The introduction to a lesson is very important for three primary reasons. First, students need to be engaged. They need to know that the material they will be learning in the lesson is interesting and important. They need to be given a reason to motivate themselves to learn it.   Second, students need to know what they are going to study— they need to know what they are expected to learn. The lesson objectives and teacher expectations should be clear from the start of the lesson. Third, students need to have their background knowledge activated. If they have ways in which to attach new knowledge to existing knowledge throughout the lesson, they will be more successful in retaining and utilizing the new knowledge.

Schemata need to be activated to draw upon the previous knowledge and learning of the ELL especially when the ELL may not have had similar experiences to the mainstream culture. The use of graphics to encourage pre-reading thought about a topic (e.g. brainstorming, web maps, and organizational charts) activates this knowledge and shows how information is organized in the students' minds. Pre-reading activities tap into this repertoire of knowledge that students bring to the classroom. This could be the knowledge acquired in the first language (language features and content) as well as cultural knowledge that would spark interest and involvement in the topic. Students are able to relate to the topic under discussion and teachers can build on this platform.

Schumm (2006) states that research has shown:

- More prior knowledge permits a reader to understand and remember more (Brown, Bransford, Ferrara, & Campione, 1983).
- Prior knowledge must be activated to improve comprehension (Bransford & Johnson, 1972).
- Failure to activate prior knowledge is one cause of poor readers (Paris & Lindauer, 1976).
- Good readers accept new information if they are convinced by an author's arguments. Likewise, they may reject ideas when they conflict with a reader's prior knowledge (Pressley, 2000).

Another approach to teach vocabulary and to build prior knowledge about the content for readers is the **language experience approach**. According to Pressley (2008) states that good readers make use of background knowledge to make inferences that is necessary for understanding a text. This helps readers cerate new knowledge from the text (*top-down processing*). In light of this view, the language experience approach supports children's concept development and vocabulary growth while offering many opportunities for meaningful reading and writing activities. It also helps in the development of shared experiences that expands children's knowledge of the world around them. In this approach, students' attention is focused on an experience in their daily life such as taking a class walk to collect leaves, blowing bubbles, making popcorn, apple picking, or experimenting with magnets. Students are involved in planning, experiencing, responding to, and recording the experience. The teacher initiates a discussion eliciting narrative from the students while providing appropriate vocabulary. In the end, the students compose oral individual or group stories which the teacher writes down and reads with students.

(See also Skill 7.1)

Skill 12.6   Analyzing the benefits of collaboration between the ESOL teacher and content-area teachers

It is important that, particularly when second language learners have multiple teachers, such as in middle or high school, that teachers communicate and collaborate in order to provide a great level consistency. It is particularly difficult for second language learners to go from one class to the next, where there are different sets of expectations and varied methods of instruction, and still focus on the more complex elements of learning language.

When students have higher levels of anxiety regarding the learning of a second language, they will be less likely to focus on the language; rather, they will be focusing on whatever it is that is creating their anxiety. This does not mean that standards and expectations should be different for these students in all classes; it simply means that teachers should have common expectations so that students know what to expect in each class and don't have to think about the differences between classes.

Another hugely important reason for teachers to collaborate, particularly with the ESOL specialists, is to ensure that students are showing consistent development across classes. Where there is inconsistency, teachers should work to uncover what it is that is keeping the student from excelling in a particular class. Collaborative or partnership teaching has long been advocated in the English language teaching profession. As Bourne (1997: 83) argues:

"Partnership Teaching is not just another term for 'co-operative teaching'. Co-operative teaching is where a language support teacher and class or subject teacher plan together a curriculum and teaching strategies which will take into account the learning needs of all pupils, trying to adjust the learning situation to fit the pupils. Partnership Teaching is more than that. It builds on the concept of co-operative teaching by linking the work of two teachers, or indeed a whole department/year team or other partners, with plans for curriculum development and staff development across the school".

There are a number of essential elements for effective collaboration between language and content-area teachers, which have been discussed elsewhere (see, for example, Davison, 1992; Hurst & Davison, 2005), including the need to establish a clear conceptualization of the task, the incorporation of explicit goals for ESL development into curriculum and assessment planning processes, the negotiation of a shared understanding of ESL and mainstream teachers' roles/responsibilities, the adoption of common curriculum planning proformas and processes, experimentation with diversity as a resource to promote effective learning for all students, the development of articulated and flexible pathways for ESL learning support, and the establishment of systematic mechanisms for monitoring, evaluation and feedback (Davison,, 2001).

Competency 13   UNDERSTAND HISTORICAL, LEGAL, AND ADMINISTRATING ASPECTS OF PROGRAMS SERVING ENGLISH LANGUAGE LEARNERS

Skill 13.1   Demonstrating knowledge of historical and current issues related to ESOL instruction

In 1961, due to the large numbers of Cuban children who migrated to Florida, Dade County Public Schools became one of the first school districts to put a major bilingual education program into action. In 1968, the Bilingual Education Act, now known as Title VII of the Elementary and Secondary Education Act (ESEA), was passed by Congress, which provided funding for all school districts to implement programs for LEP students to "participate" in academic activities.

The **Civil Rights Act of 1964** established that schools, as recipients of federal funds, cannot discriminate against ELLs: "No person in the United States shall, on the grounds of race, color, or national origin, be excluded from participation in, be denied the benefits of, or be subjected to discrimination under any program or activity receiving Federal financial assistance."

In 1970, this mandate was detailed more specifically for ELLs in the **May 25 Memorandum**: "Where inability to speak and understand the English language excludes national origin-minority group children from effective participation in the educational program offered by a school district, the district must take affirmative steps to rectify the language deficiency in order to open its instructional program to these students. The memorandum specifically addressed the practice of placing ELLs, based on their English language skills, in classes with mentally retarded students; excluding them from college preparatory classes; and notifying parents of ELLs of school activities, even if translation is required.

Since then, the Supreme Court ruled favorably in the following cases, which legally required school districts to improve educational opportunities for LEP students.

Lau v. Nichols (1974): A 1969 class action suit filed on behalf of the Chinese community in San Francisco alleged that the school district denied "equal educational opportunity" to their children because the classes the children were required to attend were not taught in the Chinese native language. The Supreme Court ruled in favor of the plaintiffs, and determined a set of requirements that academic programs must provide.

Related to Lau v. Nichols, the Office of the Department of Health, Education and Welfare created a committee of experts, who established guidelines and procedures for local educational groups serving the LEP population. The "Lau Remedies" became guidelines for all states to assist in the academic needs of LEP students; the "Lau Remedies" also provided guidelines for "exiting" LEP programs.

Per Lau v. Nichols, the Supreme Court ruled that no student shall be denied "equal access" to any academic program, due to "limited English proficiency."
In a later decision, **Castaneda v. Pickard** (filed in 1978 but not settled until 1981), a federal court established three specific criteria schools must use to determine the effectiveness of bilingual education programs:

- A program for English language learners must be based on pedagogically sound educational theory that is recognized by experts in the field

- The program must be implemented effectively with resources provided for personnel, instructional materials, and space.

- The program must produce results that indicate the language barrier is being overcome

The 1983 **A Nation at Risk** report, produced by the National Commission on Excellence in Education, concluded that the U. S. educational system was failing to meet the national need for a competitive workforce. This prompted a flurry of education reforms and initiated the National Assessment of Educational Progress (NAEP), which keeps an ongoing record of school performance. While general participation is voluntary, all schools that receive Title I money must participate. This includes low socio-economic and minority students, which includes a large percentage of ELLs. Most recently, the **No Child Left Behind (NCLB)** act established requirements that school districts must meet to continue to receive federal funds. The law has a number of requirements, but the one that has affected ELLs the most is the system of evaluating school performance based on disaggregated data. Schools can no longer rely on high-performing students to average out the low performance of language-challenged students. While the law is far from perfect, it prohibits schools from burying the low performance of any subpopulation in a school-wide average.

Skill 13.2   Applying the provisions of federal and state laws and regulations governing the delivery of ESOL instruction

The most recent reauthorization of the No Child Left Behind Act (formerly the Elementary and Secondary Education Act or ESEA) was signed into law on January 8, 2002 and is effective for a period of six years. Reauthorization of this Act was expected in 2007, but as of October 2008, Senate reauthorization has been withheld as Senators study hundreds of reform ideas. It is unlikely that the No Child Left Behind Act will be discussed until the convening of the 111th Congress in January 2009.

The NCLB Act requires schools to focus on providing quality education for students who are often overlooked by the educational system: children with disabilities, children from low-income families, non-English speakers, and African-Americans and Latinos. The following regulations, geared specifically for LEP students, were implemented in the latest revision:

- LEP students are required to be included in all academic assessments that are currently administered to other (non-LEP) students.
- When possible, the assessments must be administered in the language most likely to provide the most accurate data of the student's academic achievement and performance.
- When and if academic assessments in the student's native language cannot be obtained, the state is responsible for developing the appropriate assessment.
- In general, LEP students who have attended U.S. schools (except Puerto Rico) for at least three consecutive years must be administered assessments in English.
- The exception to this last regulation is the following: on an individual-case basis, schools have the option of permitting LEP students an extra two years before the school administers English-based assessments, if the school has determined that the LEP student's current level of English proficiency will not provide valid data..
- Parents are to be provided with a detailed report of student achievement, and explanations are provided of achievement levels.

Skill 13.3   Analyzing knowledge of the roles and responsibilities of teachers, parents and others in the education of the English language learners

Often in schools, parents, grandparents, and other people involved in children's lives, want to take a more active role in the educational process. They also all seem to have an opinion on the appropriate method for teaching students how to read. Sometimes this can lead to controversy and misunderstandings.

It is important to provide opportunities for the public to come into the school and participate in activities designed to encourage their participation in the schooling of their children . During these fun programs, it is just as important to share tidbits of information about the methodologies and strategies being implemented. In this way, the public can begin to understand the differences in ESOL instruction today in comparison to what it may have been in their native cultures when they attended school. This is often the biggest statement of concern made by adults concerning current educational trends.

Taking the time to educate parents and other family members not only helps to enhance understanding and open communication, it can also provide more support for students than the school alone would ever be able to provide.

Some strategies for educating parents and family members include:

- Bingo games where the correct answer on the Bingo board is a fact about English language instruction
- Small parent workshops offered on various topics
- Newsletter pieces or paragraphs
- Individual parent meetings
- Inviting parents to observe lessons
- Small pieces of information shared during other social times where parents are invited into the school

Communicating general information about English and appropriate English language instruction is important. It is just as important to share specific information about students with parents, other school personnel, and the community. Once the teacher has gathered sufficient information on the students, he/she must find appropriate methods to share this information with those who need the data. Again, depending on the audience, the amount and type of information shared may vary.

Some ways to share information with parents/guardians include:

- Individual parent meetings
- Small group meetings
- Regular parent updates through phone calls
- Charts and graphs of progress sent home
- Notes home

When the ESOL teacher is able to point out resources and community members who 'have made it', motivation to succeed is increased.

One of the most promising pieces of legislation to support ELL student's learning and achievement is the proposed "DREAM Act" (The Development, Relief and Education Alien Minors Act. The Dream Act is a proposed piece of federal legislation introduced in the U.S. Congress on March 26, 2009. This legislation provides the opportunity to minor aliens the opportunity to earn conditional permanent residency if they graduate from U.S. high schools, are of good moral character, and have been in the country continuously for five years or more prior to the bill's enactment.

Various community organizations provide scholarships to children of different heritages for the advancement of their education. One website portal (http://www.scholarshipsforhispanics.com/) lists possible contacts for Hispanics searching for scholarships.

Skill 13.4 Demonstrating understanding of the relationship between the ESOL program and other school programs

Content-based instruction (CBI) or "Sheltered Instruction" integrates L2 acquisition and the basic content areas of math, science, social studies, literature, etc. The most current research continues to find validity in the following:

- *Learners do not learn L2 through singular instruction in the language's rules; they learn from meaningful interaction in the language.*
- *Learners will gain proficiency in a language, only if they receive adequate input, i.e., speaking and listening start to make sense to a learner when they can build upon previous knowledge as well as understand context and cues.*
- *Although conversational fluency in L2 is a goal, speaking is not sufficient to develop the academic cognitive skills needed to learn the basic content areas.*

The goal in every classroom is for English Language Learners (ELLs) to achieve the standards in basic content areas (math, science, social studies, etc.). To accomplish this goal, ELLs must learn "academic language" which takes from five to seven years according Cummins (1993-2003). TESOL standards relating to academics state: The students will:

- *Use English to interact in the classroom*
- *Use English to obtain, process construct, and provide subject matter information in spoken and written form.*
- *Use appropriate learning strategies to construct and apply academic knowledge.*

Because ELLs typically encounter issues with vocabulary when being instructed in the content areas, it is vocabulary needs to be pre-taught and reinforced frequently to ensure the achievement of the academic language Cummins mentions.

Competency 14 **UNDERSTAND APPROACHES TO INSTRUCTION THAT ARE APPROPRIATE TO THE DIVERSITY OF THE ENGLISH LANGUAGE LEARNERS POPULATION AND THAT MEET VARIOUS STUDENT NEEDS**

Skill 14.1 **Recognizing cross- cultural and linguistic differences in communication styles (e.g., rhetorical styles, conversational styles)**

Communication in a culture is not only the language; it also involves the gestures, the facial expressions, and body stance, among other elements. For the nonverbal elements, the teacher or students can model them. Next, ask the ELLs how to do this in their culture. For example, the distance between different speakers and the way to indicate the height of a person may be different in different cultures.

In many cultures, children do not speak until called upon; in other cultures, the children may shout out an answer as soon as the question is asked. Teaching turn-taking in speaking, the use of materials, and other classroom procedures may be a year-long task.

Skill14.2 **Demonstrating knowledge of ways to acknowledge and affirm various types of diversity in the ESOL classroom, the school, and the community**

ELLs often feel as if they lose a part of themselves when faced with the complexities of learning a new language and culture. To lessen these feelings of alienation and isolation, including elements of the ELL's culture and previous knowledge only enhances the learning in the English classroom. Including culture study in the classroom may be achieved by having each student do a research project on his or her culture and report back to the class. Culture studies of this nature promote reading, writing, speaking, learning to give presentations, and creating visuals. Should there be more than one student from the same culture, pairs or small groups could be organized. Alternative types of assessment could be used to evaluate the process.

Teachers are both participants and observers in their classrooms. As such, they are in a unique position to observe what makes their students uncomfortable. By writing these observations in a teaching journal, the teacher can begin to note what activities and topics make the students in her classroom uncomfortable. Does this discomfort come from multicultural insensitivity?

Another method of **demonstrating sensitivity** is to use appropriate 'teacher talk' in the classroom. 'Wait time' for student responses differs in different cultures. Too, students who are struggling to formulate their answers may need more time than the teacher normally gives for responding. Also, if the questions are rhetorical, students may be reluctant to answer them as they see no point to such a question.

Cooperative group work is based on the premise that many cultures are more comfortable working in collaborative groups. However, while this is true, many students may feel that the teacher is the only academic authority in the classroom and as such, should answer questions, not their peers. Different students feel more comfortable with different instructional formats than others. This may be due to both cultural and individual preferences. By balancing group work with teacher-directed instruction, both points of view should be accommodated.

Literacy and reading instruction are areas where multicultural sensitivity can be increased in the classroom regardless of the level of the students. Many immigrant children arrive in the classroom with few, if any, literacy skills. They may not have had the opportunity to go to school. Others, may be fully literature and with substantial prior education. In both cases, reading materials that are culturally sensitive are necessary for the students, both native English speakers and ELLs, to have the opportunity to discuss the ways in which different cultures are alike and differ. Oral discussions of the books will provide opportunities for comprehensible input and negotiation of meaning. Research has shown that the key to any reading program is extensive reading (Day & Bamford, 1998; Krashen, 1993). Advantages include building vocabulary and background knowledge, interest in reading and improved comprehension. For the multicultural classroom, it is important to provide culturally sensitive materials. Avoid materials which distort or omit certain historical event; portray stereotyping; contain loaded words; use speech that is culturally accurate; portrays gender roles, elders and family accurately; distort or offend a student's self-image. All materials should be of high literary quality.

Show & Tell is another strategy for raising multicultural sensitivity. Students of all ages can bring in objects from their home culture and tell the class about its uses, where it is from, how it is made, and so on.

Misunderstandings can be worked into the classroom by asking students to share an incident that involved cultural misunderstanding. Questions can be asked about the nature of the misunderstanding—what was involved: words, body language, social customs, or stereotypes.

Visual/holistic versus verbal/linear-sequential: Not all learners learn in the same manner. Some students learn best through seeing information—whether written text, charts, pictures, or flow chart—visually. Other students prefer to hear the message spoken by a teacher or other students. Still other students learn best through tactile experiences, e.g. manipulating objects or equipment, creating models, or presenting material through art or drama.

According to Cassidy (2004),The holistic-analytical dimension concerns the way in which individuals tend to process information, either as a whole (holistic) or broken down into parts (analytic). Riding and Cheema (1991 in Cassidy 2004) determined that the holistic-analytical learner is commonly associated with the following terms: analytic-deductive, rigorous, constrained, convergent, formal, critical and synthetic. The verbalizer-imager concerns the way in which individuals tend to represent information either as words or as images (Cassidy 2004).

Teachers need to be aware of the different ways in which students learn so that they can prepare classroom experiences and material which encompass the different learning styles. By presenting materials through different multisensory channels, all students are given an opportunity to learn material through their preferred method learning style and to have it reinforced in other ways.

Skill 14.3   Applying knowledge of assessments to determine whether students' needs are basde on language differences and/or language disorders

Learning disabilities refer to either a physical, emotional, cognitive, or social component that severely limits what is considered to be "normal" functioning behavior. Children who fall into this category can be one or more of the following: emotionally challenged; hearing, vision, or speech impaired; learning disabled, and so on.

One similarity between second language development and learning disabilities is comprehensive diagnostic testing before placement.

Similarities:
Educators have numerous assessment tools to evaluate the proficiency level of a L2 learner. They also have various assessment tools to determine if a L1 learner has a disability, whether it is physical, emotional or learning. However, assessment tools to determine whether a L2 learner has a learning disability is not currently available. The most reliable method to date, is that of observation and interpretation.

The typical blueprint, which L2 learners seem to follow in terms of developing their pronunciation skills, can be easily confused as a learning disability, because they have difficulties with the following areas: omission, substitution, distortion and addition (Lue, 2001.) These areas are the same as encountered by some L1 learners with learning disabilities. The following are examples of the problem areas:

Omission: The L1/L2 learner omits a phoneme (the smallest unit of a word); for example, the L1/L2 learner pronounces "ar," instead of "bar."

Substitution: The L1/L2 learner substitutes a phoneme; for example, the L1/L2 learner pronounces "take," instead of "rake."

Distortion: The L1/L2 learner pronounces a phoneme incorrectly, and the sound produced is not considered normal. For example, the L1/L2 learner pronounces the phoneme "three" as "free."

Addition: The L1/L2 learner adds an additional syllable to a word. For example, a learner pronounces the word "liked" as "like-id."

A language disorder is characterized by the learner experiencing difficulties in communication and speech motor skills, and typically the learner will be noticeably behind his/her classmates in language acquisition or speech skills. The following summaries outline both the similarities and differences between second language development and language disorders. Remember that an LEP learner who has proficiency in his/her native language, but struggles in the L2 environment, is <u>not</u> considered to have a language disorder.

<u>Similarities:</u>
Some language disorders cause the learner to:

- *Mispronounce phonemes (the smallest unit of a word)*
- *Have issues with properly identifying a word in context (either verbally or non-verbally)*
- *Have difficulty associating words and their appropriate meanings*
- *Confuse proper grammatical structures*
- *Have difficulty understanding advanced vocabulary*
- *Experience difficulty following directions*

All of these characteristics of language disorders are problems experienced by the L2 learner during the process of second language acquisition, the only exception being the problem with following directions. (This falls under language disorders if the learner understands directions but is not cognitively able to follow them.) During the early stages of SLA, L2 learners experience all of the characteristics that are similar to language disorders. However, this is due primarily to unfamiliarity with the structure of the L2 language, not due to dysfunctions of communication or speech motor skills.

<u>Differences:</u>
The differences between language disorders and second language learning are more distinguishing than their similarities. First, learners experiencing problems with speech motor skills face the following challenges:

- *Unable to produce certain sounds such as "r" or "l"*
- *Have voice quality issues (such as pitch or volume)*
- *Experience "dysfluency" or stuttering*
- *Experience difficulty creating speech that is understandable to others*

Skill 14.4   Making appropriate instructional adaptations for English language learners with special educational needs (e.g., learning disabilities, giftedness) and for learners whose previous formal academic instruction has been severely interrupted

All exceptional students must have an Individualized Education Plan (IEP) developed in a meeting of the local education agency (LEA), special education teacher(s), general education teacher(s), someone to interpret assessment information, the parents, and the student (when appropriate). This IEP is a legally binding document for both the school and any teacher working with the student.

Because of the multitude of exceptionalities, it is not practical in this guide to detail all possible instructional strategies. Specific instructions for dealing with an individual's exceptionality should be spelled out in the IEP.
If no two students are alike, then no two students learn in the same way. However, certain strategies may be mentioned as good teaching practices for all teachers, especially those dealing with exceptional students.

- Teachers should use multiple instructional and assessment strategies to ensure that each student has the opportunity to learn.
- Lectures are efficient methods of transferring large amounts of information, but are limited to only one sense—hearing. Combine lectures with other instructional strategies.
- Objectives should be centered on students' interests and be relevant to their lives to maintain motivation.
- Differentiated instruction may be used to help all students achieve their maximum potential. Differentiated instruction encompasses content, process, product, and assessment.
- Students may need to prepare for test taking, because this is a stressful activity for many students with behavioral or learning disabilities. Teachers can give practice timed tests, provide study guides, leave ample space for easier reading, reduce the number of choices on multiple choice tests, use cloze tests or give a selection of choices for blank spaces in tests, give students partial outlines for essay tests, and gradually reduce the amount of scaffolding for successful students.

Skill 14.5   Selecting and applying instructional strategies appropriate to students' varied learning styles

Age
According to Ellis (1985), age does not affect the 'route' (order of) second language acquisition (SLA). Thus, both children and adults acquire language in the same order, that is, go through the same stages. With respect to rate of acquisition, teens appear to surpass both children and adults, especially in learning the grammatical system (Snow & Hoefnagel-Hohle 1978). Older learners seem to be more efficient learners, the achievement of a foreign language is strongly related to the amount of time spent on the language, and the earlier a second language is started, the better the pronunciation (Burstall et al 1974). Krashen (1982) disagrees believing instead that SLA is related to the amount of comprehensible input (i.e. the younger child will receive more comprehensible input) and that younger learners are more open emotionally to SLA. Other theorists have formulated different hypotheses about age in SLA related to affective factors. The critical period hypothesis (Penfield and Roberts (1959) states that the first 10 years are the best age for SLA as the brain retains its plasticity. After puberty, this plasticity disappears and the flexibility required for SLA is lost. Guiora et al (1972) believe that around the age of puberty, the ability to acquire native-like pronunciation of the foreign language is not longer present.

Cognitive explanations are also used to explain the effects of age on SLA. These theories believe that children are more prone to use their Language Acquisition Device (LAD) while adults are better able to use their inductive reasoning because of more fully developed cognitive faculties. Rosansky (1975) explains SLA in terms of Piaget's 'period of concrete operations'. Rosansky believes the child is more open and flexible to new language than an adult who identifies more closely with the differences in the native language and the language to be acquired. Krashen (1982) believes that adolescents and adults probably have greater access to comprehensible input than children and that this is the real causative variable and not age itself.

Level of L1 language proficiency
Children who are just beginning their education may be able to stay in the general classroom for instruction while older children may need to have specific language items (such as phonemes, syntax, pragmatics, and lexis) taught in specialized classes that take advantage of the L1 while teaching the content areas. Nevertheless, McLaughlin (1990) states the more proficient a learner is in L1, the more the learner understands about language structures and is able to use that knowledge to help make language choices when communicating in the L2

Level of L1 literacy
Cummins (1981) interdependence hypothesis claimed that the degree of knowledge and processes evident in the L1 will determine the ease of transfer to the L2. Thus, it will take a student who has L1 proficiency but an emergent reader in L1 longer to achieve proficiency in the L2 than a student who is orally proficient in his or her L1 and in L1 reading ability.

Personality

It isn't clear from research whether or not **extroversion or introversion** affects second language learning. It has been assumed that extroversion leads to better L2 acquisition, but confusing definitions in defining the different competencies make this unclear. However, it is generally assumed that extroverted students are chattier and develop more communicative competence. Entwhistle and Entwhistle (1970) found that introverted students developed better study habits and had high overall language proficiency.

Despite inconclusive evidence, **tolerance of ambiguity** is considered another trait of a good language learner. Budner (1964) developed a scale to define the language learner as one who is comfortable in novel, complex or insoluble situations (tolerance of ambiguity) or one who perceives these situations a a threat (intolerance of ambiguity). Naiman et al (1978), using Budner's scale, claimed that tolerance of ambiguity correlated to listening comprehension scores but not with imitation test scores.

Another personality trait which affects language learning is **anxiety.** MacIntyre and Gardner (1987) believe that of anxiety affects the three main stages involved in language learning: input, processing and output. Scovel (1978) studied the distinction between facilitating and debilitating anxiety. Facilitating anxiety helps the learner because the learner wants to do well and succeed while debilitating anxiety limits or holds the learner back from performing well because they cannot help themselves.

The effects of **risk taking and inhibition** similarly have conflicting evidence with regard to their effect on language learning. McClelland et al (1953) found that risk taking is necessary to rapid progress in L2. Krashen (1981) maintains that the Affective Filter develops as adolescents reach puberty; therefore, they become more self-conscious and less willing to take risks than young children. Other studies show similar results. Still, the instructor needs to be aware that most of this research was done in psychological laboratories and involves out-of-context behavior with tasks of no practical significance for language learners. Consequently, this research may be of questionable validity.

While an ELL's personality traits are probably unchangeable, the teacher can still encourage certain attitudes towards language learning that possibly could have a positive effect on the ELLs personality profile.

- Respect for the target language (TL), TL speakers, and TL culture.
- Emphasis on the practical and positive aspects of language learning.
- Confidence in the teacher is indispensible.

Preferred learning styles and modalities

A student's learning style includes cognitive, affective and psychological behaviors that indicate the learner's characteristic and consistent way of perceiving, interacting with and responding to the learning environment (Willing, 1988).

Willing (1988) identified four main learning styles used by ESL learners in Australia

- Concrete learning style: people-oriented, emotional and spontaneous
- Analytic learning style: object-orientated, capacity for making connections and inferences
- Communicative learning style: autonomous, prefers social learning, likes making decisions
- Authority-orientated learning style: defers to the teacher, does not enjoy learning by discovery, intolerant of facts that do not fit (ambiguity)

Reid (1987) identified four perceptual learning tendencies:

- Visual learning: learning mainly from seeing words in books, on the board, etc.
- Auditory learning: learning by hearing words spoken and from oral explanations, from listening to tapes or to lectures
- Kinesthetic learning: learning by experience, by being involved physically in classroom experiences
- Tactile learning: hands on learning, learning by doing, working on models, lab experiments, etc.

Educational experience

ELLs come to the United States for many different reasons: a better life, fleeing war-zones, oppressive governments, or economic difficulties. In many cases, ELLs have entered the school system in their native land and done very well there. In other cases, the ELLs have had little or no educational experience. In both cases, it is imperative that previous to or upon enrollment, assessment of the student take place—if possible in their L1. By building on their previous knowledge with regards to literacy, language, and experiences, L2 instruction will be more successful (Au, 1993, 2002; Ovando et al., 2006).

Shumm (2006) emphasizes that not only are the reading levels characteristics important, but also the differences between L1 and L2 as these may influence the assumed level of the student. Some of the questions she proposes to elicit these similarities and differences are for further evaluation of reading level characteristics:

- Is the L1 writing system logographic as is Arabic, syllabic as is Cherokee, alphabetic as is English or Greek?
- How does the L1 syntax compare with L2's?

- Are the spelling patterns phonetic with consistent grapheme-phoneme relationships (e.g. Spanish or French) or are there multiple vowel sounds (e.g. English)?
- Do students read from left to right and top to bottom in their L1?
- Are there true cognates (Spanish: instrucción and English: instruction) and false cognates (Spanish: librería <bookstore> and English: library) that will help or confuse the ELL?
- Are the discourse patterns and writing styles of L1 and L2 similar or different?
- Are questions with known answers asked (teacher questions) or are rhetorical questions (found among many working class families) asked?
- Is L1 writing style circular, with long sentences and many details (e.g. Spanish) or linear, with the minimum number of facts or supporting details needed to support the main idea (e.g. English)?

Disabilities

Students with disabilities are guaranteed an education under Public Law 94-142 of 1975. A key feature of the law is the requirement for an individualized educational program (IEP) for any student receiving special funds for special education. This said, the classification of many ELLs or 'the dumping' of ELLs in special education classes has been of concern to many educators. Those testing ELLs for placement in different classes must be certain that the test used are both reliable and valid. Reliability can be established using multiple assessment measures, objective tests, multiple raters, and clearly specified scoring criteria (Valdez-Pierce, 2003). For a test to be valid, it must first be reliable (Goh, 2004).

Learning disabilities refer to either a physical, emotional, cognitive or social component, which severely limits what is considered to be "normal" functioning behavior. Children who fall into this category can be one or more of the following: emotionally challenged, hearing, vision or speech impaired and/or learning disabled, etc.

Some of the similarities between second language development and learning disabilities are the following:

Similarities:

Educators have numerous assessment tools to evaluate the proficiency level of a L2 learner. They also have various assessment tools to determine if a L1 learner has a disability, whether it is physical, emotional or learning. However, assessment tools to determine whether a L2 learner has a learning disability is not currently available. The most reliable method to date, is that of observation and interpretation.

The typical blueprint, which L2 learners seem to follow in terms of developing their pronunciation skills, can be easily confused as a learning disability, because they have difficulties with the following areas: omission, substitution, distortion and addition (Lue, 2001.) These areas are the same as encountered by some L1 learners with learning disabilities. The following are examples of the problem areas:

Omission: The L1/L2 learner omits a phoneme (the smallest unit of a word), for example: the L1/L2 learner pronounces "_ar", instead of "bar."

Substitution: The L1/L2 learner substitutes a phoneme, for example: the L1/L2 learner pronounces "take", instead of "rake."

Distortion: The L1/L2 learner pronounces a phoneme incorrectly, and the sound produced is not considered normal, but rather it is considered a "distortion." for example: the L1/L2 learner pronounces the phoneme "three" as "free."

Addition: The L1/L2 learner adds an additional syllable to a word, making it an "addition." For example, when a learner pronounces the word "liked" as "like-id", this is an addition.

Competency 15 UNDERSTAND THE PLANNING AND MANAGEMENT OF ESOL INSTRUCTION IN A VARIETY OF SETTINGS

Skill 15.1 Demonstrating an understanding of different settings/models of ESOL instruction e.g., sheltered instruction, integrated programs) and management strategies appropriate to each

The major models of ESOL programs differ depending on the sources consulted. However, general consensus recognizes the following program models with different instructional methods used in the different programs.

Immersion Education Models
With these programs, instruction is initiated in the student's non-native language, using the second language as the medium of instruction for both academic content and the second language. Two of these models strive for full bilingualism: one is for language majority students and the other is for language minorities.

- **English Language Development (ELD) or English as a Second Language (ESL) Pull-out:** various approaches to teaching English to non-native speakers. In 1997 TESOL standards defined these approaches as intending to teach the ELL to communicate in social settings, engage in academic tasks, and use English in socially and culturally appropriate ways. Three well-known approaches to ELD or ESL are:

  o **Grammar-based ESL:** Teaches <u>about</u> the language, stressing its structure, functions and vocabulary through rules, drills, and error correction.

  o **Communication-based ESL:** Instruction in English that emphasizes <u>using </u>the language in meaningful contexts. There is little stress on correctness in the early stages and more emphasis on comprehensible input in the early stages to foster communication and lower anxiety when risk-taking.

  o **Content-based ESL:** Instruction in English that attempts to develop language skills and prepare ELLs to study grade-level content material in English. Emphasis on language, but with graded introduction to content areas, vocabulary and basic concepts.

- **Structured English immersion:** The goal is English proficiency. ELLs are pulled out for structured instruction in English so that subject matter is comprehensible. Used with sizeable groups of ELLs who speak the same language and are in the same grade level or with diverse population of language minority students. There is little or no L1 language support. Teachers use sheltered instructional techniques and have strong receptive skills in the students' native or heritage language.

- **Submersion with primary language support:** The goal is English proficiency. Bilingual teachers or aides support the minority students in each grade level who are ELLs. In small groups, the ELLs are tutored by reviewing the content areas in their primary language. The teachers use the L1 to support English content classes; ELLs achieve limited literacy in L1.

- **Canadian French immersion (language-majority students):** The goal is bilingualism in French (L2) and English (L1). The targeted population is the language-majority. Students are immersed in the L2 for the first 2 years using sheltered language instruction and then English L1 is introduced. The goal is all students of the majority language (English) becoming fluent in L2 (French).

- **Indigenous language immersion (endangered languages, such as Navajo):** Goal is bilingualism; the program is socially, linguistically and cognitively attuned to the native culture and community context. Supports endangered minority language. Develops academic skills in minority language and culture as well as in the English language and predominate culture.

Skill 15.2 Selecting appropriate ways to organize instruction for students at different ages, stages of cognitive development and proficiency levels

For beginning students, Total Physical Response by Asher (1982) allows LEPs to participate without forcing speech in the beginning of their introduction to the English language. TPR consists of the instructor issuing commands which are carried out by the students. The popular children's game Simon Says can be used after the vocabulary items have been introduced in the classroom for a slightly different way to achieve the same goals.

Krashen and Terrell (1983) developed the Natural Approach. Students are introduced to new vocabulary by different experiences. Through listening experiences, TPR, vividly colored pictures to illustrate concepts, in addition to active involvement with the pictures, learners are able to make choices, answer yes-no questions, and play games.

The Cognitive Academic Language Learning Approach (CALLA) launched by Chamot and O'Malley (1994) helps intermediate and advanced students understand and retain content area material as they are enhancing their English language skills. CALLA helps ELLs by giving instruction in the appropriate language arts (specialized vocabulary, syntax, phonology) while dealing with the different content areas. Learning strategies that emphasize critical and creative thinking skills such as problem solving, inferencing, etc., need to be taught during these lessons since they are critical to success in the mainstream classroom.

The Whole Language Approach of Goodman, Goodman, and Hood (1989) stresses the importance of developing all four language skills through an integrated approach. The Language Experience Approach is one of many different instructional strategies used to achieve this goal. Children dictate their own story based on a shared experience and then practice "reading" it until a firm grasp of the story is achieved.

ELLs must have background knowledge before they are able to succeed in content classrooms. Frequently, they are unable to relate to the experience because they are unfamiliar with the topic at hand, but if appropriate experiences are presented, ELLs are better able to deal with the situation. In order to activate the background schema Carrell and Eisterhold (1983) stress the importance of teachers activating prior knowledge in order for the ELLs to succeed in content classrooms. Backroom knowledge is activated through eliciting shared information from students before introducing new or similar topics.

Storytelling is another way of increasing language experiences for ELLs even during very early stages of language acquisition. Wajnryb (1986) claimed that storytelling has many benefits because:

- It is genuine communication.
- It is an oral tradition meant to be heard.
- It is real.
- It is sensual.
- It appeals to the affective domain.
- It is appreciated by the individual while at the same time creates a sense of community.
- It reduces anxiety by forging listening experience.
- It is pedagogically positive.

By introducing these ESOL techniques, the curriculum is adjusted without isolating the ELLs from mainstream work.

Scaffolding or supporting children of all ages consists of demonstrating, guiding, and teaching in a step-by-step process while ELLs are trying to communicate effectively ad develop their language skills (Cazden 1983; Ninio & Bruner 1976). The amount of scaffolding depends on the support needed and the individual child. It allows the ELL to assume more and more responsibility as he or she is able. Once the ELLs feel secure in their abilities, they are ready to move on to the next stage.

Educational scaffolding consists of several linked strategies including modeling academic language, contextualizing academic language using visuals, gestures, and demonstrations to help students while they are involved in hands-on learning. Some efficient scaffolding techniques are: providing direction, clarifying purpose, keeping the student on task with proposed rubrics that clarify expectations, offering suggestions for resources, supplying a lesson or activity without problems.

Tompkins (2006) identified five levels of scaffolding for learning and problem solving to show how ELLs moved from needing considerable support to the independent level where they are ready to solve problems on their own.

- **Modeling**: The instructor models orally or through written supports (a paragraph, a paper, an example) the work expected of the ELL. Projects from previous years can provide examples of the type of work expected.
- **Shared:** ELLs use their pooled knowledge of the project (and that of their teacher) to complete the assignment.
- **Interactive:** The teacher allows ELLs to question her on points that need clarification or are not understood, i.e. everyone is a learner. It is especially satisfying for the student when the teacher admits that she does not know the answer and helps the students locate it.
- **Guided:** Well posed questions, clues, reminders and examples are all ways of guiding the ELL towards the goal.
- **Independent levels:** The learner achieves independence and no longer needs educational scaffolding.

Skill 15.4   Selecting appropriate ways of grouping students for instructional purposes

Norm-referenced tests are those tests in which the test results are interpreted based upon the performance of a given group, or the norm. The 'norm group' is a large group of individuals who are similar to the group being tested. Norm referenced tests results may be compared with the norm group using the mean and standard deviations or may be reported solely based upon the actual group being tested. The latter is referred to as grading on the curve.

Criterion-referenced tests are those where the individual's test score is based upon the mastery of course content. In this type of testing, it is possible for all participants to receive the highest score regardless of how many students achieve this grade. Another category of testing refers to the first, second and third generation language tests. The first generation tests approximate grammar-translation approach to teaching language where the student is asked to perform tasks (e.g. write an essay, answer multiple choice questions). Such questions are typically devoid of context and not authentic. Second generation tests (**traditional tests**) are based on discrete points, are typically very long, and many of the items may have no connection with each other. They are often criticized precisely because of a lack of integrative language. Third generation tests (**performance-based tests**) are based upon the communicative principles and by their very nature are authentic. Examples would be listening to an airport announcement to find the time of arrival of a particular flight or writing notes from an authentic reading. The nature of the tasks requires the students to use language in an integrative form.

The strengths and weaknesses of the second and third generation tests make them suitable for different testing purposes.

There are a multitude of tests for evaluating, assessing and placing of ELLs in the appropriate programs. Each test can test a narrow range of language skills (such as discrete tests designed to measure grammar sub-skills or vocabulary).

Language tests should be chosen on the basis of the information it gives, the appropriateness of the instrument for the purpose, and the soundness of the test content. Language has over two hundred dimensions which can be evaluated, and yet most tests assess less than twelve of them. Therefore, all language testing should be done cautiously, and backed up by teacher observations, oral interviews, family life variables, and grounded in school records.

Language placement tests:
A language placement test is designed to place a student within a specific program. The school district may design its own instrument or use a standardized test.

Language proficiency tests:
These tests measure how well students have met certain standards in a particular language. The standards have been predetermined and are unrelated to any course of study, curriculum or program. These tests are frequently used to enter or exit a particular program.

Examples are:
- ACTFL Oral Proficiency Interview (OPI)
- Test of Spoken English (TSE)
- Test of English as a Foreign Language (TOEFL)
- Foreign Service Exam (FSI)
- Oral Language Proficiency Scale from Miami-Dade County Public Schools

Language achievement tests:

These tests are related directly to a specific curriculum or course of study. The test includes language sub-skills, reading comprehension, parts of speech, and other mechanical parts of the language such as spelling, punctuation and paragraphing. Examples are:

- Unit exams
- Final exams

Diagnostic language tests:

These tests are designed to identify individual students' strengths and weaknesses in languages. They are generally administered by speech therapists or psychologists in clinical settings when specific language learning problems are present.

Competency 16   UNDERSTAND METHODS OF RELATING ESOL INSTRUCTION TO STUDENTS' LIVES OUTSIDE THE CLASSROOM

Skill 16.1   Demonstrating knowledge of ways to encourage active involvement of families of English language learners in the instructional program

By advocating for the ELL student, the ESOL instructor can ensure that the students in his or her charge are able to participate in the school band, science club, math club, chess club, sports teams, and all other activities students of their age and inclination participate in.

Encouraging students and their families to make full use of public resources such as the local public library including its online resources will help them expand their own knowledge and understanding of resources available to English language learners. In addition, many libraries have after school, Saturday, or holiday programs to encourage constructive use students' time.

Museums, too, often have educational outreach programs that may be used by all citizens. Other resources such as parks and the local YMCA and YWCA (or similar organizations) offer recreational facilities to all citizens.

Skill 16.2   Applying methods of facilitating communication between the school and families of English language learners

Where possible, it is to the advantage of the ESOL instructor to be prepared to explain and if necessary suggest alternatives to the families of ELLs should educational challenges occur. Where parents are knowledgeable about their alternatives, they are better able to support their children and fully participate in the school community.

Caring teachers know that external factors can affect student behavior and performance in school.

As advocates for students, including their health and safety, teachers must be alert to issues such as eating disorders, emotional distress, suicidal tendencies, substance abuse, child abuse or neglect which can affect performance and even students' lives. While it is not the teacher's role to resolve these issues, it is their moral and legal obligation to report suspected cases of abuse to the "person in charge". Timely intervention can be the key to a better existence.

Skill 16.3   Analyzing the potential uses of home and community resources in the ESOL program

See Skill 13.3

Sample Test

Section A: (Grammar and Vocabulary)

Directions: In this part of the actual test, you will hear and read a series of short speeches of nonnative speakers of English. Then you will be asked questions about each student's problems in grammar or vocabulary in the recorded speech. You will be allotted ample time to answer the questions.

(N.B. Xamonline does not provide recorded material with this book. If possible, have someone read the questions in this section to you. You may hear the selection only once.)

1. **Listen to an ESOL student talk about his experience with living in the United States. *(Easy)***

    (Taped excerpt)

    My name Rimas and I'm from Charleston. I live there for four years…

    The verb "live" in the second sentence is incorrect with respect to

    A. Tense

    B. Gender

    C. Person

    D. Number

2. **Listen to an ESOL student talking about her friend's boyfriend.**

    (Easy)

    (Taped excerpt)

    Your boyfriend is too handsome.

    The adverb "too" is incorrect with regards to

    A. Usage

    B. Form

    C. Spelling

    D. Word order

3. **Listen to an ESOL student talking about an email he received.**

    (Easy)

    (Taped excerpt)

    Just look at this email from my teacher. He says I was missing my last two tests.

    The verb "was missing" is incorrect with regards to

    A. Tense.

    B. Agreement.

    C. Subjunctive.

    D. Number.

4. **Listen to an ESOL student talking about her parents.**

   (Average)
   (Taped excerpt)

   My parents deal with much problems every day.

   The word "much" is incorrect with regard to the use of _____ nouns.

   A. Count/no count

   B. Regular/irregular

   C. Collective

   D. Compound

5. **Listen to an ESOL student talking about love and marriage.**

   (Rigorous)
   (Taped excerpt)

   Many people are afraid of falling in love and to marry.

   The words "to marry" are incorrect with regard to

   A. Tense

   B. Agreement

   C. Parallel structure

   D. Adverbial format

6. **Listen to an ESOL student talking to her friend about English customs.**

   (Average)

   (Taped excerpt)

   One must always be on time.

   "One" refers to

   A. You.

   B. They.

   C. The listener.

   D. The speaker.

7. **Listen to an ESOL student talking about dolphins.**

   (Average)

   (Taped excerpt)

   Dolphins are interesting mammals. They give milk, but it lives in the ocean.

   The word "it" is incorrect with respect to

   A. Reference.

   B. Antecedent.

   C. Gender.

   D. Class.

8. **Listen to an ESOL student talking to her friend about life in the United States.**

(Average)

(Taped excerpt)

I think that's a little obtuse. After all, things are different here.

The word "obtuse" means

A. Sharp
B. Complicated.
C. Happy.
D. Insensitive.

9. **Listen to an ESOL student talking about her boss' reorganization of office procedures.**

(Easy)

(Taped excerpt)

My boss just reorganized our ordering system. As far as I can see, it makes no sense. It has neither rhyme nor reason.

The word "or" in the last sentence is incorrect with regards to

A. Parallel structure.
B. Usage.
C. Form.
D. Person.

10. **Listen to an ESOL student talking about meeting her friend at the airport.**

(Easy)

(Taped excerpt)

I'll go to pick up Jonathan. She gets in at three.

The word "she" is incorrect with regards to

A. Agreement.
B. Gender.
C. Person.
D. Number.

Section B (Pronunciation)

Directions: In this part of the actual test, you will hear and read a series of short speeches of nonnative speakers of English. Then you will be asked questions about each student's problems in pronunciation in the recorded speech. You will not be asked to evaluate the student's grammar or vocabulary usage. To help you answer the questions, the speech will be played a second time. You will be allotted ample time to answer the questions.

(N.B. XAMonline does not provide recorded material with this book. If possible, have someone read the questions in this section to you. You may hear the selection only twice.)

11. Listen to an ESOL student reading aloud the following sentence.

(Rigorous)

(Taped excerpt)

He went on a ship. (Student pronounces "ship" as [shi:p].

The error in pronunciation in the word "ship" indicates a problem with

A. Diphthongs.

B. Primary cardinal vowels.

C. Triphthongs.

D. Allophones.

12. Listen to an ESOL student reading aloud the following sentence.

(Rigorous)

(Taped excerpt)

Fish and chips. (Student pronounces "and" as [aend].)

The error in pronunciation in the word "and" indicates a problem with

A. Elision.

B. Assimilation.

C. Phonemes.

D. Weakness.

13. Listen to an ESOL student reading aloud the following sentence.

(Rigorous)

(Taped excerpt)

Today's Sunday. I am going to church. (Student pronounces "church" as [shət□].)

The error in pronunciation of the word "church" indicates problems with

A. Affricatives.

B. Plosives.

C. Laterals

D. Glides.

14. Listen to an ESOL student reading aloud the following sentence.

    (Average)

    (Taped excerpt)

    What a glorious day. Look at that sky. (Student pronounces "sky" as [ski].)

    The error in pronunciation of the word "sky" indicates problems with

    A. Short vowels.

    B. Diphthongs.

    C. Triphthongs.

    D. Long vowels.

15. Listen to an ESOL student reading aloud the following sentence.

    (Average)
    (Taped excerpt)

    What are we going to see? (Student pronounces "are" as [är].)

    The error in pronunciation of the word "are" indicates problems with

    A. Schwa
    B. Stress.
    C. Suprasegmentals.
    D. Prosody.

16. Listen to an ESOL student reading aloud the following sentence.
    (Rigorous)
    (Taped excerpt)

    I've three sisters. (Student pronounces "three" as [tri:].)

    The error in pronunciation of the word "three" indicates problems with

    A. Labials.
    B. Affricatives.
    C. Palatals.
    D. Fricatives.

17. Listen to an ESOL student reading aloud the following sentence.

    (Rigorous)

    (Taped excerpt)

    Judy read two scripts before giving them to me to study. (Student pronounces "scripts" as [skrɪpts].)

    The error in pronunciation of the word "scripts" indicates problems with

    A. Fricatives.

    B. Assimilation.

    C. Linking.

    D. Elision.

18. Listen to an ESOL student reading aloud the following sentence.

   (Average)
   (Taped excerpt)

   Susan bought him an elegant watch. (Student pronounces and emphasizes each word.)

   The error in speaking the sentence indicates problems with

   A. Intonation.

   B. Linking sounds.

   C. Pitch.

   D. Neutrals.

19. Listen to an ESOL student reading aloud the following sentence.

   (Average)
   (Taped excerpt)

   Marjorie has lots of problems with her parents. She is such a rebel. (Student pronounces "rebel" as [re/BEL].)

   The error in pronunciation of the word "rebel" indicates problems with

   A. Pitch.

   B. Reduction.

   C. Stress.

   D. Rhythm.

20. Listen to an ESOL student reading aloud the following sentence.

   (Average)
   (Taped excerpt)

   What do you like about that movie? (Student pronounces "movie" with a rising voice.)

   The error in pronunciation of the word "movie" indicates problems with

   A. Pitch.

   B. Stress.

   C. Function words.

   D. Intonation.

Section C (Writing Analysis)
Directions: In this part of the test, you will read a series of short writings samples produced by nonnative speakers of English. You will be asked to identify the errors in the students' writing. Therefore, before taking the test, you should be familiar with the writing of nonnative speakers who are learning English.

(N.B. There is no recorded material for this section of the test.)

Questions 21-23 are based on the following excerpt from an essay describing the student's experience with language learning.

Teachers in my country of foreign languages are well qualified to carry out their duties properly. They must possess a degree from a university language program if they wishes to teach in high school or below. Many also teach in universities, but many need a post-graduate degree. Teachers should be very good at pronouncing the words so their students can imitate they.

21. In the first sentence, the error is in the relative order of

(Average)

A. A noun and an adjective.
B. The direct and indirect objects.
C. The subject and object.
D. The prepositional phrases.

22. The second sentence contains an error in the

(Average)

A. Agreement between the pronoun and verb
B. Pronoun antecedent and referent
C. Structure of the subordinate clause
D. Order of the sentence elements.

23. The last sentence contains an error in the

(Average)

A. Noun and an adjective
B. Direct and indirect objects
C. Subject and the object
D. Pronoun form

Questions 24-26 are based on an excerpt from an essay describing the student's hometown.

My hometown is Cali, Colombia located in the Cauca River Valley. Cali is surrounded with mountains and cut in half by the Cauca River. Colombians eat many kinds of tropical fruits and vegetables. My favorite dish is a chicken soup with plantains, cassava, potatoes and beef. My mother served this with rice. Visitors can do many exciting things in Cali: riding horses, to swim, and to play tennis. We want you to come.

24. In sentence 5, the correct form of the verb 'served' should be:

(Average)

A. Serves.
B. Serving.
C. Is serving.
D. Has served

25. In the sixth sentence, there is an error in the

(Rigorous)

A. Verb tense.
B. Parallel structure.
C. Punctuation.
D. Subject and object.

26. In the last sentence, the error is in the

(Rigorous)

A. Infinitive.
B. Objective pronoun.
C. Pronoun shift.
D. Subject pronoun.

Questions 27-30 are based on the following excerpt from an essay describing the student's future plans.

When I finish my studies in the United States, I would return to my country. I like the United States very much, but I miss my families. If I was a rich person, I could do what I want, but I cannot. I must take care of my mother and my brothers. Maybe before a foreigner could stay in the United States and get a job, but today, I believe I have a better future in my personal country.

27. In the first sentence, the error is in the

(Rigorous)

A. Pronouns.
B. Conditional tense.
C. Placement of the subordinate clause.
D. Verb tense.

28. In the second sentence, the error is in the

(Average)

A. Noun and verb agreement.
B. Use of a plural noun.

C. Preposition.
D. Direct object.

29. In the third sentence, the error is in the

(Rigorous)

A. Verb.
B. Pronoun agreement.
C. Subjunctive.
D. Word choice.

30. In the last sentence, the error is in the

(Rigorous)

A. Punctuation.
B. Subject pronoun.
C. Direct object.
D. Word choice.

31. "Bite" and "byte' are examples of which phonographemic differences?

(Average)

A. Homonyms.
B. Homographs.
C. Homophones.
D. Heteronyms.

32. Words which have the same spelling or pronunciation, but different meanings are:

(Easy)

A. Homonyms.
B. Homographs.
C. Homophones.
D. Heteronyms.

33. If you are studying "morphemic analysis", then you are studying:

(Easy)

A. The smallest unit within a language system to which meaning is attached.
B. The root word and the suffix and/or prefix.
C. The way in which speech sounds form patterns.
D. Answers A and B only.

34. The study of morphemes may provide the student with:

(Average)

A. The meaning of the root word.
B. The meaning of the phonemes.
C. Grammatical information.
D. All of the above.

35. Which one of the following is NOT included in the study of "semantics"?

(Rigorous)

A. Culture.
B. The definition of individual words and meanings.
C. The intonation of the speaker.
D. Meaning which is "stored" or "inherent", as well as "contextual".

36. If you are studying "pragmatics", then you are studying:
(Easy)

A. The definition of individual words and meanings.
B. How context impacts the interpretation of language.
C. Meaning which is "stored" or "inherent", as well as "contextual".
D. All of the above.

37. If you are studying "syntax", then you are studying:
(Average)

A. Intonation and accent when conveying a message.
B. The rules for correct sentence structure.
C. The definition of individual words and meanings.
D. The subject-verb-object order of the English sentence.

38. Language learners seem to acquire syntax:
(Average

A. At the same rate in L1 and L2.
B. Faster in L2 than L1.
C. In the same order regardless of whether it is in L1 or L2.
D. In different order for L1.

39. Arrange the following sentences, written by ELLs, to show the order of acquisition of negation, ranging from least to most

Sentence 1: Kim didn't went to school.
Sentence 2: No school. No like.
Sentence 3: Kim doesn't like to go to school.
(Average)

A. Sentence 1, Sentence 2, Sentence 3.
B. Sentence 3, Sentence 2, Sentence 1.
C. Sentence 1, Sentence 3, Sentence 2.
D. Sentence 2, Sentence 1, Sentence 3.

40. When referring to discourse in the English language, which is the most important principal for successful oral communication?
(Average)

A. Taking "turns" in conversation.
B. Choice of topic.
C. The setting or context of the conversation...
D. Empty language.

41. Polite discourse includes phrases such as 'How are you?' or 'See you later' as examples of:
(Easy)

  A. CALP
  B. A skit
  C. Empty language.
  D. Formal speech.

42. The sentence: "The bus was late and he was late, but John still managed to catch it." Is an example of a _____ .
(Rigorous)

  A. Simple sentence.
  B. Compound sentence.
  C. Complex sentence.
  D. Compound-complex sentence.

43. The vocabulary word "ain't" has been used for /am not/, /is not/, and /has not/. It is an example of _____.
(Rigorous)

  A. A dialect.
  B. How language evolves.
  C. Socio-economic effects on language.
  D. A southern drawl.

44. Which one of the following is not a factor in people changing their register? The:
(Average)

  A. Relationship between the speakers.
  B. Formality of the situation.
  C. Attitude towards the listeners and subject.
  D. Culture of the speakers.

45. "Maria is a profesora" is an example of:
(Rigorous)

  A. Dialect
  B. Inter-language
  C. Code-switching
  D. Formulaic speech

46. English has grown as a language primarily because of:
(Easy)

  A. Wars/technology and science
  B. Text messaging/immigrants
  C. Immigrants/technology and science
  D. Contemporary culture/wars

47. **Identify the major factor in the spread of English.**
   (Easy)

   A. The invasion of the Germanic tribes in England.
   B. The pronunciation changes in Middle English.
   C. The extension of the British Empire.
   D. The introduction of new words from different cultures.

48. **Communication involves specific skills such as:**
   (Average)

   A. Turn-taking.
   B. Silent period
   C. Lexical chunks
   D. Repetition

49. **Interlanguage is best described as:**
   (Easy)

   A. A language characterized by overgeneralization.
   B. Bilingualism.
   C. A language learning strategy.
   D. A strategy characterized by poor grammar.

50. **"The teacher 'writted' on the whiteboard" is an example of:**
   (Easy)

   A. Simplification.
   B. Fossilization.
   C. Inter-language.
   D. Overgeneralization.

51. **The creation of original utterances is proof that the L2 learner is:**
   (Rigorous)

   A. Recalling previous patterns.
   B. Mimicking language chunks.
   C. Applying knowledge of L1 to L2.
   D. Using cognitive processes to acquire the L2.

52. **Social factors influence second language learning because:**
   (Average)

   A. Age determines how much one learns.
   B. Gender roles are predetermined.
   C. Social status is important in the ELLs ability to perform well in the learning situation.
   D. Many ELLS cannot ignore their social conditions.

53. **Schumman's acculturation model does not assert:**
    (Rigorous)

    A. L1 language learners want to acquire L2 in order to remain in their new culture.
    B. The target language group accepts L1 learners in their culture.
    C. L1 and L2 groups both wish for the L1 to assimilate into the culture.
    D. L1 and L2 advocates disagree on the sharing of social services and conveniences.

54. **Simplification means:**
    (Easy)

    A. Adding 'ed' to irregular verbs as a way to use the past tense.
    B. Stating 'I have a house beautiful in Miami' for 'I have a beautiful house in Miami'.
    C. Hispanics pronouncing words like 'student' as 'estudent'.
    D. Asking someone if 'You like?' instead of 'Do you like this one?'

55. **In the statement "Peter, come here, please", the correct stress would be on:**
    (Easy)

    A. PEter; PLEASE.
    B. peTER; HERE.
    C. peTER: COME.
    D. peTER; PLEASE.

56. **To change the imperative sentence "Come here, Susan." to a polite request, the correct form is:**
    (Easy)

    A. Would you come here, Susan?
    B. Do you come here, Susan?
    C. Can you come here, Susan?
    D. Will you come here, Susan?

57. **L1 and L2 learners follow the approximately the same order in learning a language. Identify the correct sequence from the options below.**
    (Easy)

    A. Silent period, experimental speech, private speech, lexical chunks, formulaic speech.
    B. Silent period, private speech, lexical chunks, formulaic speech, experimental speech.
    C. Private speech, lexical chunks, silent period, formulaic speech, experimental speech.
    D. Private speech, silent period, lexical chunks, formulaic speech, experimental speech.

58. When referring to a wealthy person as a "fat cat", the speaker is using a/an:
(Easy)

  A. Cognate.
  B. Derivational morpheme.
  C. Phrase.
  D. Idiom.

59. When the teacher is correcting a student's language, the teacher should:
(Easy)

  A. Carefully correct all mistakes.
  B. Consider the context of the error.
  C. Confirm the error by repeating it.
  D. Repeat the student's message but correcting it.

60. A teacher who asks the ELL if he or she has finished the task really means 'Finish the assignment.' This is an example of:
(Easy)

  A. Synonyms.
  B. Pragmatics.
  C. Culture in the classroom.
  D. Body language.

61. According to Krashen and Terrell's Input Hypothesis, language learners are able to understand:
(Average)

  A. Slightly more than they can produce.
  B. The same as they speak.
  C. Less than they speak.
  D. Lots more than they speak.

62. Bilingualism of ELLs can be greatly improved by:
(Average)

  A. A block schedule
  B. Community's appreciation of the L2
  C. Speaking L2 in the school
  D. Interference occurring between L1 and L2

63. Experts on bilingualism recommend:
(Average)

  A. The use of the native language (mother tongue) until schooling begins.
  B. Reading in L1 while speaking L2 in the home.
  C. Exposing the child to both languages as early as possible.
  D. Speak the language of the school as much as possible.

64. The affective domain affects how students acquire a second language because:
(Rigorous)

A. Learning a second language may make the learner feel vulnerable.
B. The attitude of peers and family is motivating.
C. Motivation is a powerful personal factor.
D. Facilitative anxiety determines our reaction to competition and is positive.

65. Research shows that error correction in ELLs is a delicate business. Which of the following contributes to learning? Correction of:
(Rigorous)

A. Semantic errors.
B. Grammatical errors.
C. Pronunciation.
D. All written work errors.

66. ESOL instruction frequently requires the teacher to change her instruction methods. One of the most difficult may be the:
(Rigorous)

A. Wait time.
B. Establishment of group work.
C. Show and tell based on different cultures.
D. Extensive reading time.

67. Community Language Learning requires the members of the group and the teacher to:
(Rigorous)

A. Use cue cards and pictures.
B. Trust each other.
C. Use self-expression to expand their knowledge.
D. React physically to a command

68. If the teacher circulates around the room answering questions and asking others, she is demonstrating which level(s) of scaffolding:
(Rigorous)

A. Modeling.
B. Interactive.
C. Guided.
D. Independent.

69. Ms. Mejia is concerned that her ELLs learn to write correctly in English. She:
(Average)

A. Dictates sentences with the week's spelling words.
B. Plays Hangman to reinforce spelling of the words.
C. Reads stories using vocabulary the ELLs need for BICS or CALP.
D. Sends extra work home for the ELLs to practice.

70. Angela needs help in English. Her teacher suggested several things Angela can do to improve her learning strategies. One of the following is <u>not</u> a socioaffective learning strategy.
(Easy)

A. Read a funny book.
B. Work cooperatively with her classmates.
C. Ask the teacher to speak more slowly.
D. Skim for information.

71. An ESOL teacher who encourages her students to keep track of their progress in English Language Learning is stimulating which learning strategy?
(Rigorous)

A. Metacognitive
B. Affective
C. Cognitive
D. Social

72. Advanced TPR might include:
(Average)

A. Rapid fire commands.
B. More advanced vocabulary.
C. Funny commands.
D. All of the above.

73. Which of the following is <u>not</u> a step in the Language Experience Approach?
(Rigorous)

A. Students draw a picture to represent something personal about an experience.
B. Students dictate their story to the teacher.
C. The teacher reads the story revising where necessary.
D. The story is read in later days as a follow-up activity.

74. Content-based instruction suggests LEP students need an additional 5-7 years to pick-up academic language. During this time period, content area teachers should <u>not</u>:
(Average)

A. Correct the LEP's oral language mistakes.
B. Speak more slowly, enunciation.
C. Demonstrate new materials using various strategies to increase input.
D. Check frequently for comprehension by asking students to explain what was said to a classmate or back to the teacher.

75. The researcher most identified with the importance of working through problems to obtain a solution and to learn a foreign language is:
(Rigorous)

A. Asher.
B. Krashen & Terrell.
C. Postovsky.
D. Prabhu.

76. Which of the following instructional approaches emphasizes LEPs working on content?
(Average)

A. TPR.
B. The Natural Approach.
C. CALLA.
D. The Communicative Approach.

77. The Schema Theory of Carrell & Eisterhold suggests that for learning to take place, teachers must:
(Rigorous)

A. Integrate content areas with ESOL techniques.
B. Emphasize all four language skills.
C. Present comprehensible input in a meaningful context.
D. Relate new materials to previous knowledge.

78. According to Cummins four levels of difficulty, the high school math teacher whose ELLs work on standard workbook problems, is using _____ materials.
(Average)

A. Level 1: Cognitively undemanding / Context-embedded
B. Level 2: Cognitively undemanding / Context-reduced
C. Level 3: Cognitively demanding / Context-embedded
D. Level 4: Cognitively demanding / Context-reduced

79. Identify one of the following methods of dealing with fossilization as not appropriate.
(Average)

A. Ignore mistakes that do not interfere with meaning.
B. Work on items such as ending /s/ for third person singular in written work.
C. Teacher (or aide) corrects all the errors in the
D. papers.
E. Dictating correct sentences of patterns frequently used incorrectly by ELLs.

80. **Identify one method of adapting general education instruction to ELLs.**
(Average)

   A. Providing extra listening materials (e.g. CD-Rom's of stories).
   B. Arrange homogenous work groups.
   C. Using an English dictionary.
   D. Using grade-level storybooks.

81. **Using a 'video split':**
(Rigorous)

   A. Is effective with science experiments.
   B. Is an information gap activity.
   C. Forces ELLs to use L2.
   D. Creates awareness of authentic language.

82. **When using instructional technology (e.g. videos, DVDs, or CDs) in ESOL classes, the instructor should:**
(Rigorous)

   A. Play the entire piece to build listening skills.
   B. Frequently stop to check on comprehension.
   C. Quiz the ELLs for comprehension after listening.
   D. Block the captions on the video.

83. **Using asynchronous applications teachers can:**
(Average)

   A. Design coursework for students to complete by specific dates.
   B. Send instant messages (IMs).
   C. Enhance student interaction.
   D. Increase student's interest.

84. **CALL gives ELLs the opportunity to:**
(Rigorous)

   A. Practice writing skills in chatrooms.
   B. Receive instructor feedback during the class.
   C. See each other through video conferencing.
   D. All of the above.

85. **Kroonenberg believes the value of CMC:**
(Rigorous)

   A. For instructors, is that they can integrate video and audio into instruction.
   B. Is that its authoring software tools help teachers prepare course materials.
   C. Lies in its ability to imitate live conversation.
   D. Is achieved by cultural authenticity.

86. Teachers looking for reading comprehension software for young ELLs should look for: *(Average)*

   A. Illustrated vocabulary lists, which are presented before the story.
   B. A text which is read accompanied by animation.
   C. Interactive vocabulary words.
   D. A page for the students to illustrate their retelling of the story at the end.

87. The most appropriate ESOL strategy for readers who do not read in their L1 is to: (Average)

   A. Postpone reading until the ELLs acquire intermediate oral language proficiency.
   B. Teach cognates and high frequency words.
   C. Develop literacy in L1 first.
   D. Use pull-out reading support in L2.

88. ELLs who are beginning to write in L2 demonstrate which traits: *(Average)*

   A. Word-order problems, lack of variety in vocabulary, use different sentence patterns.
   B. Write 3 or more paragraphs with run-on sentences, little vocabulary above basic level, limited organization.
   C. Limited vocabulary, use one or two sentence patterns, write only a few sentences.
   D. Ask for translation of vocabulary at times, good variety of sentence patterns, write a paragraph or more.

89. All of the following strategies except one are recommended to promote emergent literacy. It is: *(Average)*

   A. Teacher reads oversized books carefully pointing to each word as she reads.
   B. Mother Goose rhymes illustrated around the room.
   C. Spelling lists for homework practice.
   D. Word wall with words listed under each beginning letter.

90. Incorporating prior knowledge into L2 learning does **not**:

   (Average)

   A. Permit readers to learn and remember more.
   B. Cause poor readers.
   C. Help readers to evaluate new arguments.
   D. Improve comprehension.

91. Freire's research states:
(Average)

A. Critical literacy provides a means for individual to identify with the nature of social conditions and change them.
B. Critical literacy is an investigation into the motives and goals of an author or speaker.
C. Readers are critical consumers of information received.
D. Oppressed people obtain power through education and knowledge.

92. An English teacher included a unit on Shakespeare's Romeo and Juliet in her programming. To promote critical literacy, she could have her students:
(Average)

A. Provide a list of pre-reading questions for discussion.
B. Use a flow-chart to outline the plot.
C. Compare the story of Prince Charles and Princess Diana to Romeo and Juliet.
D. Show the movie and provide comprehension questions.

93. Instruction to promote fluency includes:
(Average)

A. Developing writing and reading skills separately.
B. Explicit study of vocabulary lists.
C. Role plays, phonics instruction, journal writing.
D. Learning only the specific language for the task at hand.

94. Young children are often considered better language learners than older children or adults. However, older children or adults may be able to progress more rapidly in reading instruction because:
(Rigorous)

A. They have more worldly experience to help them understand the texts.
B. Their vocabulary concepts in L2 are less developed.
C. They have more language learning experience.
D. Phonics is the same whether in L1 or L2.

95. **Teachers of ELL students should be able to use both verbal and non-verbal communication techniques. Identify each of the following as Verbal (V) or Non-verbal Speech (NV).**
(Average)

A. _____ Mime
B. _____ Initiating
C. _____ Paraphrasing
D. _____ Gestures
E. _____ Summarizing
F. _____ Acting out a sequence of events
G. _____ Questioning
H. _____ Listening

96. **Technology and globalization have placed increased demands on schools. One disappointment of ELL education has been:**
(Rigorous)

A. ELLs often succeed in the corporate ranks.
B. Bilingual skills are in great demand.
C. Too many ELLs make little use of their language skills.
D. ELLs frequently return to their native lands.

97. **Culture and cultural differences:**
(Average)

A. Must be addressed by the teacher in the ELL classroom by pointing out cultural similarities and differences.
B. Should be the starting point for learning about how culture affects the ELLs attitude towards education.
C. Positively affects how well ELLs perform in the language classroom.
D. May have strong emotional influence on the ELL learner.

98. **Pierre arrived in the U. S. in 2005. He has been living with his uncle and aunt who are well assimilated into the U.S. culture. Pierre misses his parents and brothers. He finds his high school studies fairly easy and his classmates lazy. He is worried about his goal of becoming a professional soccer player and doesn't understand why he can't have wine with his meals when he eats out with his aunt and uncle. In which stage of assimilation is Pierre?**
(Average)

A. Honeymoon stage.
B. Hostility stage.
C. Humor stage.
D. Home stage.

99. Upon arrival in a new country, immigrants frequently show signs of _____ in order to get a job.
    (Easy)

    A. Assimilation.
    B. Acculturation.
    C. Transculturation.
    D. Accommodation.

100. Which of the following accommodations may be allowed for ELLs during assessment?
    (Average)

    A. Giving extra time.
    B. Asking proctor to explain certain words or test items.
    C. Paraphrasing the prompt.
    D. May use an English-heritage translating dictionary.

101. Which of the following is <u>not</u> an acceptable alternative assessment strategy for ELLs?
    (Average)

    A. Portfolios.
    B. Observation.
    C. Self-assessment.
    D. Essay writing.

102. Which method is the most appropriate method for dealing partially with cultural bias in tests?
    (Rigorous)

    A. Translate the tests previous to the actual exam.
    B. Provide pictures and graphics during the test.
    C. Administer practice tests with time limits.
    D. Provide a study guide and give test orally.

103. When testing for an ELLs level of English proficiency, which minor accommodation is appropriate?
    (Rigorous)

    A. Extra time may be allowed.
    B. Using the ELLs portfolio.
    C. Recitation.
    D. Providing translation of prompts as needed for understanding.

104. Before coming to the U.S., Sven, an 11-grade student took the TOEFL. This is a _____ test.
    (Easy)

    A. Language proficiency.
    B. Language achievement.
    C. Language placement.
    D. Diagnostic language.

105. A 5th grader has completed one year in the ESOL program but does not seem to make progress. Which of the following might indicate a learning disability?
(Rigorous)

A. Frequently code switches.
B. Needs extra time to answer questions.
C. Is able to decode successfully but has comprehension difficulties.
D. Dropping of the final consonants of words.

106. An ELL student may pronounce /free/ instead of /three/. This is an example of:
(Rigorous)

A. Omission.
B. Substitution.
C. Distortion.
D. Addition.

107. Which of the following is indicative of a language disorder rather than a L2 developmental issue?
(Rigorous)

A. Difficulty in identifying words in context.
B. Inability to produce grammatically correct sentences.
C. Dropping of specific word endings.
D. Speech is difficult for others to understand.

108. Which of the following should be done prior to initiating a formal referral process for an ELL with possible learning disabilities?
(Rigorous)

A. A vision and hearing test.
B. A language diagnostic test.
C. Documentation of at least 1 intervention.
D. Consultation with principal about ELL's progress.

109. Which of the following is a possible sign of the gifted ELL student?
(Average)

A. Normal development according to parental interview.
B. Speech delayed in L2.
C. Seems to solve logic problems with difficulty.
D. High academic performance in L1.

110. An ELL suspected of having learning difficulties:
(Rigorous)

A. May present behavioral differences when asked to produce written work.
B. Might demonstrate the ability to learn quickly.
C. Should be analyzed for up to 10 weeks using ESOL techniques.
D. May demonstrate the ability to solve problems not dependent on English.

111. **Identify the correct order for assessment of ELLs with exceptionalities. (Rigorous)**

   A. English language assessment, language proficiency assessment, language for assessment.
   B. Speech and language assessment, language for assessment, English language assessment.
   C. Language for assessment, speech and language assessment, language proficiency.
   D. Language proficiency assessment, speech and language assessment, English language assessment.

112. **Which of the following instructional strategies would not be appropriate for ELLs with exceptionalities? (Rigorous)**

   A. Use of texts adapted to students disability.
   B. Practice testing opportunities.
   C. Differentiated instruction.
   D. Lectures.

113. **In a school where numerous ELL students of the same language group are present, the most efficient way to ensure conformity with the Consent Decree may be: (Rigorous)**

   A. Pull-out classes for science and math
   B. Mainstream content instruction with pull-out for Language Arts instruction.
   C. Mainstream instruction for Language Arts, science and math with tutorials in problem areas.
   D. Pull-out classes for Language Arts and science, mainstream for math.

114. **The No Child Left Behind Act established: (Rigorous)**

   A. Title I funds are available only if the schools participate in National Assessment of Education Progress.
   B. Bilingual programs must be effective and established three criteria.
   C. High performance children cannot be used to average out low performing ELLs.
   D. Schools must form and convene assessment committees.

115. *Bilingual Schooling and the Miami Experience* documents Miami-Dade County's:
(Easy)

A. Experience in scaffolding.
B. As pioneers in ESL in the U.S.
C. As leading investigators in EFL in the U.S.
D. Reaction to cultural differences.

116. In schools with large immigrant populations of diverse origin, the most commonly used model is:
(Average)

A. Submersion.
B. Pull-out ESL.
C. SDAIE.
D. Transition.

117. Widdowson's definition of 'use' and 'usage' is well demonstrated in which of the following models?
(Rigorous)

A. Canadian French Immersion and Miami-Dade Count models
B. Submersion with primary language support
C. Content-based ESL and indigenous language immersion
D. Communication-based ESL and Grammar-based ESL.

118. Based on Title III of the No Child Left Behind Act, schools are required to include ELLs in state-mandated testing:
(Rigorous)

A. In mathematics and science after 2 years of enrollment.
B. In English language arts, math, and science after 2 years enrollment.
C. In English language arts and math after enrollment.
D. In mathematics with 1 year of enrollment.

119. The No Child Left Behind Act requires schools to:
(Rigorous)

A. Give assessment in English if the LEP has received 3 years of schooling in the US (except for Puerto Rico).
B. Measure school districts by status.
C. Inform parents of the school's evaluation.
D. Includes LEPs in all academic assessments.

120. In Lau v Nichols (1974), the Supreme Court ruled that:
(Rigorous)

    A. School districts may not continue education programs that fail to produce positive results for ELLs.

    B. Prohibited sexual harassment in any school activity on or off campus.

    C. Students were denied an 'equal' education.

    D. Prohibited discrimination against students and employers based on race, ethnicity, national origins, disability, or marital status.

Answer Key

1. A
2. A
3. A
4. A
5. C
6. A
7. B
8. D
9. C
10. B
11. B
12. A
13. A
14. B
15. A
16. D
17. D
18. B
19. C
20. D
21. D
22. A
23. D
24. A
25. B
26. C
27. B
28. B
29. C
30. D
31. C
32. B
33. D
34. C
35. A
36. B
37. B
38. C
39. D
40. A
41. C
42. D
43. B
44. D

45. C
46. C
47. C
48. A
49. C
50. D
51. D
52. D
53. D
54. D
55. A
56. A
57. B
58. D
59. D
60. B
61. A
62. B
63. C
64. D
65. A
66. A
67. C
68. B
69. C
70. D
71. A
72. D
73. C
74. A
75. D
76. C
77. D
78. D
79. C
80. A
81. B
82. B
83. A
84. D
85. D
86. B
87. C
88. C
89. C
90. D

91. D
92. C
93. C
94. A
95. A NV, B V, C V, D NV, E V, F NV, G V, H V
96. C
97. D
98. B
99. D
100. D
101. D
102. C
103. A
104. A
105. C
106. C
107. D
108. A
109. D
110. D
111. B
112. D
113. D
114. C
115. C.
116. B
117. C
118. D
119. A
120. C

Rigor Table

	Easy %20	Average Rigor %40	Rigorous %40
Question #	1, 2, 3, 9, 10, 32, 33, 36, 41, 46, 47, 49, 50, 54, 55, 56, 57, 58, 59, 60, 70, 99, 104, 115.	4, 6, 7, 8, 14, 15, 18, 19, 20, 21, 22, 23, 24, 28, 31, 34, 37, 38, 40, 44, 48, 52, 61, 62, 63, 69, 72, 74, 76, 78, 79, 80, 83, 86, 87, 88, 89, 90, 91, 92, 93, 95, 97, 98, 100, 101, 109, 116.	5, 11, 12, 13, 16, 17, 25, 26, 27, 29, 30, 35, 39, 42, 43, 45, 51, 53, 64, 65, 66, 67, 68, 71, 73, 75, 77, 81, 82, 84, 85, 94, 96, 102, 103, 105, 106, 107, 108, 110, 111, 112, 113, 114, 117, 118, 119, 120.

RATIONALES

Section A: (Grammar and Vocabulary)
Directions: In this part of the actual test, you will hear and read a series of short speeches of nonnative speakers of English. Then you will be asked questions about each student's problems in grammar or vocabulary in the recorded speech. You will be allotted ample time to answer the questions.

(N.B. Xamonline does not provide recorded material with this book. If possible, have someone read the questions in this section to you. You may hear the selection only once.)

1. **Listen to an ESOL student talk about his experience with living in the United States.** *(Easy)*

   (Taped excerpt)

   My name Rimas and I'm from Charleston. I live there for four years...

   The verb "live" in the second sentence is incorrect with respect to

   A. Tense
   B. Gender
   C. Person
   D. Number

   Answer: A. Tense.
   The pronoun 'I' is not gender specific, so it may be used for both male and female people. Rimas is singular, therefore, 'I live' for first person singular is correct in both person and number. However, when discussing permanent situations, the present perfect tense 'have lived' is the correct tense. Thus, option A is the correct answer.

2. **Listen to an ESOL student talking about her friend's boyfriend.**
   (Easy)

   (Taped excerpt)

   Your boyfriend is too handsome.

   The adverb "too" is incorrect with regards to

   A. Usage
   B. Form
   C. Spelling
   D. Word order

   Answer: A. Usage.
   The form, spelling and word order are all correct. Therefore, option A must be the incorrect form. The correct usage, in this case, would be the adverb 'very'.

3. **Listen to an ESOL student talking about an email he received.**
   (Easy)
   (Taped excerpt)

   Just look at this email from my teacher. He says I was missing my last two tests.

   The verb "was missing" is incorrect with regards to

   A. Tense.
   B. Agreement.
   C. Subjunctive.
   D. Number.

   Answer: A. Tense.
   In this case, 'was missing' is correct with regards to agreement and number. The subjunctive is not indicated. So, the correct answer is A. The simple past, 'missed' is used for reported speech when the speaker is reporting an event in the present.

4. **Listen to an ESOL student talking about her parents.**
   (Average)

   (Taped excerpt)

   My parents deal with much problems every day.

   The word "much" is incorrect with regard to the use of _____ nouns.

   A. Count/no count
   B. Regular/irregular
   C. Collective
   D. Compound

   Answer: A. Count/no count.
   Regular/irregular adjectives such as 'good/the best' do not concern the word 'much'. Much is an adjective, not a collective or compound noun. Much is used with uncountable nouns. Therefore, A count/no count nouns is the correct option. Many, which is used with plural countable nouns, would be the correct word.

5. **Listen to an ESOL student talking about the love and marriage.**
   (Rigorous)

   (Taped excerpt)

   Many people are afraid of falling in love and to marry.

   The words "to marry" are incorrect with regard to

   A. Tense
   B. Agreement
   C. Parallel structure
   D. Adverbial format

   Answer: C. Parallel structure.
   Gerunds have neither tense nor agreement elements. A gerund is a verbal used as a noun not an adverb. Thus, option C is the correct one. As the sentence contains both a gerund and an infinitive, one should be changed to make both elements have the same structure. The question is phrased so that 'to marry' should be changed to 'marrying'.

6. **Listen to an ESOL student talking to her friend about English customs.**
   (Average)

   (Taped excerpt)

   One must always be on time.

   "One" refers to

   A. You.
   B. They.
   C. The listener.
   D. The speaker.

   Answer: A. You.
   In this question, 'one' refers to a general 'you'. American English generally uses 'you' instead of 'one', however both are correct. The correct option is A.

7. **Listen to an ESOL student talking about dolphins.**
   (Average)
   (Taped excerpt)

   Dolphins are interesting mammals. They give milk, but it lives in the ocean.
   The word "it" is incorrect with respect to

   A. Reference.
   B. Antecedent.
   C. Gender.
   D. Class

   Answer: B. Antecedent.
   Gender and class refer to the type of pronoun chosen to be used in oral speech or a written text. 'Dolphins' is a 'referent' not a 'reference'. The word 'it' is a pronoun which should refer back to its antecedent 'dolphins'. The antecedent 'dolphins' is a countable, plural noun indicating that any pronoun referring back to it should also be plural. Answer B is the correct option for the statement.

8. **Listen to an ESOL student talking to her friend about life in the United States.**
   (Average)

   (Taped excerpt)

   I think that's a little obtuse. After all, things are different here.

   The word "obtuse" means

   A. Sharp
   B. Complicated.
   C. Happy.
   D. Insensitive.

   Answer: D. Insensitive.

9. **Listen to an ESOL student talking about her boss' reorganization of office procedures.**
   (Easy)

   (Taped excerpt)

   My boss just reorganized our ordering system. As far as I can see, it makes no sense. It has neither rhyme or reason.

   The word "or" in the last sentence is incorrect with regards to

   A. Parallel structure.
   B. Usage.
   C. Form.
   D. Person.

   Answer: C. Form.
   Parallel structure, usage, and person do not apply in this case since 'neither/nor' is a correlative conjunction. With the negative 'neither', the correct form is 'nor'. 'Or' is used with the positive 'either'. The correct answer is C.

10. **Listen to an ESOL student talking about meeting her friend at the airport.**
    (Easy)
    (Taped excerpt)

I'll go to pick up Jonathan. She gets in at three.

The word "she" is incorrect with regards to

A. Agreement.
B. Gender.
C. Person.
D. Number.

Answer: B. Gender.
The third person singular of the verb 'get' is 'gets', so the agreement of number and person are correct. The incorrect gender has been used as Jonathan is a male name. Thus, 'he' would be the correct pronoun. Option B is the best selection.

Section B (Pronunciation)
Directions: In this part of the actual test, you will hear and read a series of short speeches of nonnative speakers of English. Then you will be asked questions about each student's problems in pronunciation in the recorded speech. You will not be asked to evaluate the student's grammar or vocabulary usage. To help you answer the questions, the speech will be played a second time. You will be allotted ample time to answer the questions.

(N.B. XAMonline does not provide recorded material with this book. If possible, have someone read the questions in this section to you. You may hear the selection only twice.)

11. **Listen to an ESOL student reading aloud the following sentence.**
    (Rigorous)
    (Taped excerpt)

He went on a ship. (Student pronounces "ship" as [shi:p].

The error in pronunciation in the word "ship" indicates a problem with

A. Diphthongs.
B. Primary cardinal vowels.
C. Triphthongs.
D. Allophones.

Answer: B. Primary cardinal vowels.
Diphthongs refer to a combination of two phonemes that glide together. Triphthongs are vowel sounds in which three vowels are sounded in a sequence, such as 'fire' or 'flower'. Allophones refer to sounds regional speakers make. Thus, answer B is the best option since the pronunciation of the vowel 'i' is in question.

12. Listen to an ESOL student reading aloud the following sentence.
  (Rigorous)
  (Taped excerpt)

Fish and chips. (Student pronounces "and" as [aend].)

The error in pronunciation in the word "and" indicates a problem with

A. Elision.
B. Assimilation.
C. Phonemes.
D. Weakness.

Answer: A. Elision.
Assimilation refers to a phoneme being spoken differently when it is near another phoneme. This is more common in rapid, casual speech. Weakness in English is defined as reduction, assimilation and elision. The question refers to a specific type of weakness—elision where two phonemes disappear to create a 'n' in typical speech. The best option is A.

13. Listen to an ESOL student reading aloud the following sentence.
  (Rigorous)
  (Taped excerpt)

Today's Sunday. I am going to church. (Student pronounces "church" as [shət□].)

The error in pronunciation of the word "church" indicates problems with

A. Affricatives.
B. Plosives.
C. Laterals
D. Glides.

Answer: A. Affricatives.
English has six plosive consonants. Only the consonant classified as a lateral alveolar in English is the 'l'. Glides refer to diphthongs where sound does not remain consonant but glides from one sound to another. Affricatives are stop consonants that are released slowly into a period of fricative noise such as the 'ch' in church. The correct option is A.

14. Listen to an ESOL student reading aloud the following sentence.
(Average)
(Taped excerpt)

What a glorious day. Look at that sky. (Student pronounces "sky" as [ski].

The error in pronunciation of the word "sky" indicates problems with

A. Short vowels.
B. Diphthongs.
C. Triphthongs.
D. Long vowels.

Answer: B. Diphthongs.
Short vowels are those in such words as "pat, pet, pit, pot, and put. Long vowels are those such as 'take, mete, mike, toke, and mute'. Triphthongs are vowel sounds in which three vowels are sounded in a sequence, such as 'fire' or 'flower'. The diphthong [skaɪ]) should be used instead of the pure long vowel 'i'. Therefore, B is the correct choice.

15. Listen to an ESOL student reading aloud the following sentence.
(Average)
(Taped excerpt)

What are we going to see? (Student pronounces "are" as [är].)

The error in pronunciation of the word "are" indicates problems with

A. Schwa
B. Stress.
C. Suprasegmentals.
D. Prosody.

Answer: A. Schwa.
The speaker does not have problems in stress at the word or sentence level. Suprasegmentals refer to teaching the 'big picture' or the characteristics that extend over entire utterances as versus teaching individual elements such as how to pronounce the letter 'd'. Stress is an element of prosody; the other is intonation. The schwa /ə/ is used as a symbol to represent an 'emptiness' in pronunciation. For example, the 'er' at the end of many words is pronounced using the schwa. The correct answer is A.

16. **Listen to an ESOL student reading aloud the following sentence.**
 (Rigorous)
 (Taped excerpt)

I've three sisters. (Student pronounces "three" as [tri:].)

The error in pronunciation of the word "three" indicates problems with

A. Labials.
B. Affricatives.
C. Palatals.
D. Fricatives.

Answer: D. Fricatives.
Labials refer to a group of consonants in which the lips form their distinctive sound. The palatals are those sounds made by raising the front of the tongue towards the hard palate. Affricatives are stop consonants that are released slowly into a period of fricative noise such as the 'ch' in church. The 'th' sound in English is represented as a dental fricative and may be voiced or voiceless. The 'th' sound in three is voiced and represented by the /ð/.

17. **Listen to an ESOL student reading aloud the following sentence.**
 (Rigorous)
 (Taped excerpt)

Judy read two scripts before giving them to me to study. (Student pronounces "scripts" as [skrɪpts].)

The error in pronunciation of the word "scripts" indicates problems with

A. Fricatives.
B. Assimilation.
C. Linking.
D. Elision.

Answer: D. Elision.
Assimilation refers to a phoneme being spoken differently when it is near another phoneme. This is more common in rapid, casual speech. Lin.king refers to sounds that join with the following sounds to produce a 'linked' sound, such as Alice in Wonderland where the 'c' becomes an 's' and links with 'in' /sin/. Weakness in English is defined as reduction, assimilation and elision. The question refers to a specific type of weakness—elision where three phonemes appear together. The most likely scenario is that native speakers would drop the middle phoneme 't' , pronouncing the word as [skrɪps]. The best option is A.

18. **Listen to an ESOL student reading aloud the following sentence.**
   (Average)
   (Taped excerpt)

   Susan bought him an elegant watch. (Student pronounces and emphasizes each word.)

   The error in speaking the sentence indicates problems with

   A. Intonation.
   B. Linking sounds.
   C. Pitch.
   D. Stress-timed.

   Answer: B. Linking sounds.
   Intonation concerns the tone pattern of speech and is produced by changing the vocal pitch. Pitch refers to the rising / falling pattern of the voiced speech. Some linguists refer to English as a stress-timed language whereas many other languages, e.g. Spanish, are syllable-timed. If a student pronounces and emphasizes each word, then the student has trouble with linking sounds as 'bought him' would surely be linked as /boughim/.

19. **Listen to an ESOL student reading aloud the following sentence.**
   (Average)
   (Taped excerpt)

   Marjorie has lots of problems with her parents. She is such a rebel. (Student pronounces "rebel" as [re/BEL].)

   The error in pronunciation of the word "rebel" indicates problems with

   A. Pitch.
   B. Reduction.
   C. Stress.
   D. Rhythm.

   Answer: C. Stress.
   Pitch refers to the high or low tone of the voice. Stress refers to accent. Reduction has to do with the speaker reducing certain phonemes in order to produce simpler, easier to pronounce utterances. Rhythm is the sound pattern achieved through stressed and unstressed syllables. The stress or accent of certain words in English change their grammatical function in an utterance. The word [re/BEL] is a verb. The correct word should be [REB/el] a noun. C is the best option.

20. Listen to an ESOL student reading aloud the following sentence.

(Average)
(Taped excerpt)

What do you like about that movie? (Student pronounces "movie" with a rising voice.)

The error in pronunciation of the word "movie" indicates problems with

A. Pitch.

B. Stress.

C. Function words.

D. Intonation.

Answer: D. Intonation.
Pitch refers to the high or low tone of the voice. Stress refers to accent. Grammatical or function words are words which show how other words and sentences relate to each other, e.g. in, the, which, etc. Intonation concerns the pattern of pitch and stress changes uttered in a phrase or a sentence. The best option is D.

Section C (Writing Analysis)
Directions: In this part of the test, you will read a series of short writings samples produced by nonnative speakers of English. You will be asked to identify the errors in the students' writing. Therefore, before taking the test, you should be familiar with the writing of nonnative speakers who are learning English.

(N.B. There is no recorded material for this section of the test.)

Questions 21-23 are based on the following excerpt from an essay describing the student's experience with language learning.

Teachers in my country of foreign languages are well qualified to carry out their duties properly. They must possess a degree from a university language program if they wishes to teach in high school or below. Many also teach in universities, but many need a post-graduate degree. Teachers should be very good at pronouncing the words so their students can imitate they.

21. In the first sentence, the error is in the relative order of

(Average)

A. A noun and an adjective.
B. The direct and indirect objects.
C. The subject and object.
D. The prepositional phrases.

Answer: D. The prepositional phrases.
The error lies in the order of the first two prepositional phrases. The sentence should read 'Teachers of foreign languages in my country...'. Answer D is the correct option.

22. The second sentence contains an error in the

(Average)

A. Agreement between the pronoun and verb.
B. Pronoun antecedent and referent.
C. Structure of the subordinate clause.
D. Order of the sentence elements.

Answer: A. Agreement between the pronoun and verb.
The sentence should read 'if they wish to teach in high school or below.' Therefore the correct option is A.

23. The last sentence contains an error in the

(Average)

A. Noun and an adjective
B. Direct and indirect objects
C. Subject and the object
D. Pronoun form

Answer: D. Pronoun form.
In the last sentence, the antecedent of 'they' is 'their students'. Therefore, the objective form should be used in the phrase 'so their students can imitate them.' The correct option is D.

Questions 24-27 are based on an excerpt from an essay describing the student's hometown.

My hometown is Cali, Colombia located in the Cauca River Valley. Cali is surrounded with mountains and cut in half by the Cauca River. Colombians eat many kinds of tropical fruits and vegetables. My favorite dish is a chicken soup with plantains, cassava, potatoes and beef. My mother served this with rice. Visitors can do many exciting things in Cali: riding horses, to swim, and to play tennis. We want you to come.

24. In sentence 5, the correct form of the verb 'served' should be:

(Average)

A. Serves.
B. Serving.
C. Is serving.
D. Has served

Answer: A. Serves.
The author is discussing how his mother serves the chicken soup—always. Therefore, the simple present tense is used. Selection A is the correct option.

25. In the sixth sentence, there is an error in the

(Rigorous)

A. Verb tense.
B. Parallel structure.
C. Punctuation.
D. Subject and object.

Answer: B. Parallel structure.
The items in this series ('...: riding horses, to swim, and to play tennis') should all have the same structure. They should all be gerunds or infinitives but not mixed together. Thus, Answer B is the correct answer.

26. In the last sentence, the error is in the

(Rigorous)

A. Infinitive.
B. Objective pronoun.
C. Pronoun shift.
D. Subject pronoun.

Answer: C. Pronoun shift.
The author may confuse his readers if he changes his writing from 'his' point of view to that of Colombians in general. He should be careful to use 'First person' throughout his paragraph and not change to 'We'. Therefore, C is the correct option.

Questions 27-30 are based on the following excerpt from an essay describing the student's future plans.

When I finish my studies in the United States, I would return to my country. I like the United States very much, but I miss my families. If I was a rich person, I could do what I want, but I cannot. I must take care of my mother and my brothers. Maybe before a foreigner could stay in the United States and get a job, but today, I believe I have a better future in my personal country.

27. In the first sentence, the error is in the

(Rigorous)

A. Pronouns.
B. Conditional tense.
C. Placement of the subordinate clause.
D. Verb tense.

Answer: B. Conditional tense.
The adverbial clause 'When I finish…' expresses present time and should be followed by a simple future tense to complete the speaker's utterance. The conditional 'would' is not correct. Option B is the correct selection.

28. In the second sentence, the error is in the

(Average)

A. Noun and verb agreement.
B. Use of a plural noun.
C. Preposition.
D. Direct object.

Answer: B. Use of a plural noun.
The student probably has only one 'family'; so 'but I miss my families' would be incorrect. Answer B is the best option.

29. In the third sentence, the error is in the

(Rigorous)

A. Verb.
B. Pronoun agreement.
C. Subjunctive.
D. Word choice.

Answer: C. Subjunctive.
Though it is becoming more acceptable to say 'I was', careful educated speakers still use the subjunctive form 'I were'. Selection C is the best option.

30. In the last sentence, the error is in the

(Rigorous)

A. Punctuation.
B. Subject pronoun.
C. Direct object.
D. Word choice.

Answer: D. Word choice.
There are many ways for the speaker to express his 'personal country' in a more acceptable way. Some of these would be 'my country', 'my native country', or 'my country of origin'. The correct option is D.

31. "Bite" and "byte' are examples of which phonographemic differences?

(Average)

A. Homonyms.
B. Homographs.
C. Homophones.
D. Heteronyms.

Answer: C. Homophones.
'Homonyms' is a general term for words with two or more meanings. Homographs are two or more words with the same spelling or pronunciation, but have different meanings. Heteronyms are two or more words that have the same spelling but different meanings and spellings. Homophones are words that have the same pronunciation, but different meanings and spellings and the correct response.

32. Words which have the same spelling or pronunciation, but different meanings are:

(Easy)

A. Homonyms.
B. Homographs.
C. Homophones.
D. Heteronyms.

Answer: B. Homographs.
See explanation given after question 3.

33. If you are studying "morphemic analysis", then you are studying:

(Easy)

A. The smallest unit within a language system to which meaning is attached.
B. The root word and the suffix and/or prefix.
C. The way in which speech sounds form patterns.
D. Answers A and B only.

Answer: D. Answers A and B only.
The study of the way in which speech sounds form patters is called phonology. The smallest unit within a language system to which meaning is attached is a morpheme. The root word and the suffix and/or prefix are components of morphemes and basic to the analysis of a word. Therefore, both A and B are necessary for the study of morphemic analysis so the correct answer is D.

34. The study of morphemes may provide the student with:
(Average)

A. The meaning of the root word.
B. The meaning of the phonemes.
C. Grammatical information.
D. All of the above.

Answer: C. Grammatical information.
The meaning of the root word comes from its source or origin, and the meaning of phonemes relates to its sound. The correct answer is C which gives grammatical information to the student rather than (e.g. prepositions or articles)

35. Which one of the following is NOT included in the study of "semantics"?

(Rigorous)

A. Culture.
B. The definition of individual words and meanings.
C. The intonation of the speaker.
D. Meaning which is "stored" or "inherent", as well as "contextual".

Answer: A. Culture.
Since semantics refers to the definition of individual words and meanings, the intonation of the speaker, and meaning which is "stored" or "inherent", as well as "contextual", option A is the best response.

36. If you are studying "pragmatics", then you are studying:

(Easy)

A. The definition of individual words and meanings.
B. How context impacts the interpretation of language.
C. Meaning which is "stored" or "inherent", as well as "contextual".
D. All of the above.

Answer: B. How context impacts the interpretation of language.
The definition of individual words and meanings refers to semantics. Meaning which is 'stored or "inherent", as well as contextual refers to the lexicon of a language. The best option is B as pragmatics refers to studies how context impacts the interpretation of language.

37. If you are studying "syntax", then you are studying:
(Average)

A. Intonation and accent when conveying a message.
B. The rules for correct sentence structure.
C. The definition of individual words and meanings.
D. The subject-verb-object order of the English sentence.

Answer: B. The rules for correct sentence structure.
The intonation and accent used when conveying a message refer to pitch and stress. The definition of individual words and meanings is semantics. The subject-verb-object order of the English sentence refers to is the correct order for most English sentences, but the rules for correct sentence structure refers to syntax, so B is the best option.

38. Language learners seem to acquire syntax:

(Average)

A. At the same rate in L1 and L2.
B. Faster in L2 than L1.
C. In the same order regardless of whether it is in L1 or L2.
D. In different order for L1.

Answer: C. In the same order regardless of whether it is in L1 or L2.
All language learners must progress through the same hierarchical steps in their language learning process. They go from the least to the most complicated stages regardless of whether it is in the L1 or L2.

39. Arrange the following sentences, written by ELLs, to show the order of acquisition of negation, ranging from least to most
Sentence 1: Kim didn't went to school.
Sentence 2: No school. No like.
Sentence 3: Kim doesn't like to go to school.
(Average)

A. Sentence 1, Sentence 2, Sentence 3.
B. Sentence 3, Sentence 2, Sentence 1.
C. Sentence 1, Sentence 3, Sentence 2.
D. Sentence 2, Sentence 1, Sentence 3.

Answer: D. Sentence 2, Sentence 1, Sentence 3.
The correct order is D.

40. When referring to discourse in the English language, which is the most important principal for successful oral communication?
(Average)

A. Taking "turns" in conversation.
B. Choice of topic.
C. The setting or context of the conversation...
D. Empty language.

Answer: A. Taking "turns" in conversation.
For discourse to be successful in any language, a set of ingrained social rules and discourse patterns must be followed. The choice of topic and the setting or context of the conversation are important elements of discourse in English, but not the most important ones. Empty language refers to discourse perfunctory speech that has little meaning but is important in social exchanges. In oral English discourse, taking "turns" is primordial. The correct option would be A.

41. Polite discourse includes phrases such as 'How are you?' or 'See you later' as examples of:

(Easy)

A. CALP
B. A skit
C. Empty language.
D. Formal speech.

Answer: C. Empty language.
The two statements are examples of empty language which is used in polite discourse but carries very little meaning.

42. The sentence: "The bus was late and he was late, but John still managed to catch it." Is an example of a _____ .
(Rigorous)

A. Simple sentence.
B. Compound sentence.
C. Complex sentence.
D. Compound-complex sentence.

Answer: D. Compound-complex sentence.
The first sentence contains two independent clauses 'The bus was late and he was late' as well as 'John still managed to catch it.' The first clause is also a compound clause with two independent clauses 'The bus was late' 'he was late'. Thus our sentence becomes compound-complex.

43. The vocabulary word "ain't" has been used for /am not/, /is not/, and /has not/. It is an example of _____.
(Rigorous)

A. A dialect.
B. How language evolves.
C. Socio-economic effects on language.
D. A southern drawl.

Answer: B. How language evolves.
The word "ain't" first came into usage in the 17th century when many different contracted forms of speech began to appear. For reasons unknown, in the U.S. it became unacceptable (as did many other contracted forms) but remains in regular usage in rural, working class, and inner city people's speech. In the 17th century it was used instead of has not/have not (*an't/ain't*), in the 18th century /*an't*/ was used for *am not, are not,* and *is not*. It is an excellent example of B--how language evolves.

44. **Which one of the following is <u>not</u> a factor in people changing their register? The:**
    (Average)

    A. Relationship between the speakers.
    B. Formality of the situation.
    C. Attitude towards the listeners and subject.
    D. Culture of the speakers.

    Answer: D. Culture of the speakers.
    People change their register depending on the relationship between the speakers, the formality of the situation, and the e attitudes towards the listeners and the subject. Answer D—culture of the speakers is not a reason for people to change their register.

45. **"Maria is a profesora" is an example of:**
    (Rigorous)

    A. Dialect
    B. Inter-language
    C. Code-switching
    D. Formulaic speech

    Answer: C. Code-switching.
    Dialect is any form or variety of a spoken language peculiar to a region, community, social group, etc. Inter-language is the language spoken by ELLs that is between their L1 and L2. Formulaic speech refers to speech that is ritualistic in nature and perhaps used for social politeness rather than information.

    Sociolinguistics is a very broad term used to understand the relationship between language and people including the phenomenon of people switching languages during a conversation. One person may switch languages when a word is not known in the other language. Option C is the correct option.

46. English has grown as a language primarily because of:
   (Easy)

   A. Wars/technology and science
   B. Text messaging/immigrants
   C. Immigrants/technology and science
   D. Contemporary culture/wars

   Answer: C. Immigration/technology and science.
   While all of the options have influenced the growth of English, new immigrants continually adding new words to the language is the most influential factor. The second largest body of new words comes from technology and science making Option C the best option.

47. Identify the major factor in the spread of English.
   (Easy)

   A. The invasion of the Germanic tribes in England.
   B. The pronunciation changes in Middle English.
   C. The extension of the British Empire.
   D. The introduction of new words from different cultures.

   Answer: C. The extension of the British Empire.
   The sun never set on the British Empire during the 19th century causing English to spread all over the world. (The predominance of English in data banks—an estimated 80-90 percent of the world's data banks are in English—keeps English as the foremost language in the world today.) Thus, Option C is the correct one.

48. Communication involves specific skills such as:
   (Average)

   A. Turn-taking.
   B. Silent period
   C. Lexical chunks
   D. Repetition

   Answer: A. Turn-taking.
   The silent period refers to a pre-production period observed before the ELL begins communicating. Lexical chunks are blocks of language used in everyday speech and writing. Repetition is used as a clarification technique or a stalling technique before the ELL is ready to proceed. All are part of the language acquisition process. There are many skills involved in communication, but the only one listed is turn-taking.

49. Interlanguage is best described as:

(Easy)

A. A language characterized by overgeneralization.
B. Bilingualism.
C. A language learning strategy.
D. A strategy characterized by poor grammar.

Answer: C. A language learning strategy.
Interlanguage occurs when the second language learner lacks proficiency in L2 and tries to compensate for his or her lack of fluency in the new language. Three components are overgeneralization, simplification, and L1 interference or language transfer. Therefore, answer A is only one component of interlanguage making option C the correct answer.

50. "The teacher 'writted' on the whiteboard" is an example of:
(Easy)

A. Simplification.
B. Fossilization.
C. Inter-language.
D. Overgeneralization.

Answer: D. Overgeneralization.

In this case, the ELL has tried to apply the rule of /ed/ endings to an irregular verb to form the past tense verb, i. e. he has used 'overgeneralization' to create an incorrect verb form. The correct answer is D.

51. The creation of original utterances is proof that the L2 learner is:
(Rigorous)

A. Recalling previous patterns.
B. Mimicking language chunks.
C. Applying knowledge of L1 to L2.
D. Using cognitive processes to acquire the L2.

Answer: D. Using cognitive processes to acquire the L2.
Recalling previous patterns, mimicking language chunks, and applying knowledge of L1 to L2 do not demonstrate organization and direction of second language acquisition. The ELL has not integrated the L2 into his or her thought processes. When the ELL is able to form rules, they are able to understand and create new utterances. Selection D is the correct option.

52. **Social factors influence second language learning because:**
    (Average)

    A. Age determines how much one learns.
    B. Gender roles are predetermined.
    C. Social status is important in the ELLs ability to perform well in the learning situation.
    D. Many ELLS cannot ignore their social conditions.

    Answer: D. Many ELLs cannot ignore their social conditions.
    Motivation whether a trait (state) or a state (instrumental) is probably the most powerful element in the acquisition of a second language. Without family or community support, the ELL may be under tremendous pressure and feel threatened by the new language. For them to succeed, they must do so at considerable personal sacrifice.

53. **Schumman's acculturation model does not assert:**
    (Rigorous)

    A. L1 language learners want to acquire L2 in order to remain in their new culture.
    B. The target language group accepts L1 learners in their culture.
    C. L1 and L2 groups both wish for the L1 to assimilate into the culture.
    D. L1 and L2 advocates disagree on the sharing of social services and conveniences.

    Answer: D. L1 and L2 advocates disagree on the sharing of social services and conveniences.
    Schumman's acculturation model asserts the first three affirmations. Option D is the fourth affirmation, but should read 'L1 and L2 advocates agree to share social services and conveniences'. Thus as written, Option D is the correct option.

54. Simplification means:

(Easy)

A. Adding 'ed' to irregular verbs as a way to use the past tense.
B. Stating 'I have a house beautiful in Miami' for 'I have a beautiful house in Miami'.
C. Hispanics pronouncing words like 'student' as 'estudent'.
D. Asking someone if 'You like?' instead of 'Do you like this one?'

Answer: C. Students were denied and 'equal' education.
Answer A refers to Castaneda v Pickard (1981). Answer B refers to Title IX of the Education Amendments of 1972. Answer D was covered in Florida Educational Equity Act of 1984. Only Option C refers to Lau v Nichols (1974).

Simplification is a common learner error involving simplifying the language where the correct structures have not been internalized. In this case, the correct question form has not been acquired though the ELLs meaning is clear.

55. In the statement "Peter, come here, please", the correct stress would be on:
(Easy)

A. PEter; PLEASE.
B. peTER; HERE.
C. peTER: COME.
D. peTER; PLEASE.

Answer: A. PEter; PLEASE.

56. To change the imperative sentence "Come here, Susan." to a polite request, the correct form is:
(Easy)

A. Would you come here, Susan?
B. Do you come here, Susan?
C. Can you come here, Susan?
D. Will you come here, Susan?

Answer: A. Would you come here, Susan?
In polite requests with 'you' as the subject, either 'would you' or 'will you' have the same meaning. Would you is used more often and considered politer. However, the degree of politeness is determined by the tone of the speaker's voice.

57. L1 and L2 learners follow the approximately the same order in learning a language. Identify the correct sequence from the options below.
(Easy)

A. Silent period, experimental speech, private speech, lexical chunks, formulaic speech.
B. Silent period, private speech, lexical chunks, formulaic speech, experimental speech.
C. Private speech, lexical chunks, silent period, formulaic speech, experimental speech.
D. Private speech, silent period, lexical chunks, formulaic speech, experimental speech.

Answer: B: Silent period, private speech, lexical chunks, formulaic speech, experimental speech.
The correct order is B.

58. **When referring to a wealthy person as a "fat cat", the speaker is using a/an:**
(Easy)

A. Cognate.
B. Derivational morpheme.
C. Phrase.
D. Idiom.

Answer: D: Idiom.
Idioms are new meanings assigned to words that already have a meaning in a language. The expression 'fat cat' literally means a cat that is fat. However, it has become an idiomatic way to say someone is a wealthy person.

59. **When the teacher is correcting a student's language, the teacher should:**
(Easy)

A. Carefully correct all mistakes.
B. Consider the context of the error.
C. Confirm the error by repeating it.
D. Repeat the student's message but correcting it.

Answer: D. Repeat the student's message but correcting it.
To carefully correct all mistakes a student makes would raise the affective filter and probably cause the student to hesitate before speaking. Considering the context of the error gives the teacher insight into the student's learning, but isn't a method of correction. To confirm the error by repeating it would suggest to the student that his or her utterance was correct and not good practice. The best option is D which corrects the error but in a way that shows the student the correct form without embarrassing him or her.

60. A teacher who asks the ELL if he or she has finished the task really means 'Finish the assignment.' This is an example of:
(Easy)

A. Synonyms.
B. Pragmatics.
C. Culture in the classroom.
D. Body language.

Answer: B. Pragmatics.
'Synonyms' refers to two words that mean the same. The statement 'finish the assignment' has no particular significance and the teacher is not using 'body language' when she makes a simple statement. The best option is B pragmatics where the teacher is implying that she can see that it has not been finished and is issuing a command to do so.

61. According to Krashen and Terrell's Input Hypothesis, language learners are able to understand:
(Average)

A. Slightly more than they can produce.
B. The same as they speak.
C. Less than they speak.
D. Lots more than they speak.

Answer: A. Slightly more than they can produce.
Krashen and Terrell's Input Hypothesis ($i + 1$) states that instruction should be at a level slightly above the language learner's production level. In this way the learner will have the basis with which to understand but will have to figure out the unknown language in context.

62. **Bilingualism of ELLs can be greatly improved by:**
   (Average)

   A. A block schedule
   B. Community's appreciation of the L2
   C. Speaking L2 in the school
   D. Interference occurring between L1 and L2

   Answer: B. Community's value of the L2.
   Motivation is always a key factor in language learning and when an ELL
   has community support for second language/cultural learning, bilingualism
   is greatly enhanced. Option B is the best option.

63. **Experts on bilingualism recommend:**
   (Average)

   A. The use of the native language (mother tongue) until schooling begins.
   B. Reading in L1 while speaking L2 in the home.
   C. Exposing the child to both languages as early as possible.
   D. Speak the language of the school as much as possible.

   Answer: C. Exposing the child to both languages as early as possible.
   Research on bilingualism suggests that children should be exposed to
   both languages from birth where possible for maximum bilingual benefit.

64. The affective domain affects how students acquire a second language because:
(*Rigorous*)

   A. Learning a second language may make the learner feel vulnerable.
   B. The attitude of peers and family is motivating.
   C. Motivation is a powerful personal factor.
   D. Facilitative anxiety determines our reaction to competition and is positive.

Answer: A. Learning a second language may make the learner feel vulnerable.
The affective domain refers to the full range of human feelings and emotions that come into play during second language acquisition. Learning a second language may make the learner vulnerable because they may have to leave their comfort zone behind. This can be especially difficult for adults who are used to being 'powerful' or 'in control' in their profession, but also affects children and teens. Option A is the best selection here.

65. Research shows that error correction in ELLs is a delicate business. Which of the following contributes to learning? Correction of:
(*Rigorous*)

   A. Semantic errors.
   B. Grammatical errors.
   C. Pronunciation.
   D. All written work errors.

Answer: A. Semantic errors.
The correction of semantic errors leads to increased vocabulary and L2 learning. All other options have been proven to be ineffective.

66. ESOL instruction frequently requires the teacher to change her instruction methods. One of the most difficult may be the: **(Rigorous)**

A. Wait time.
B. Establishment of group work.
C. Show and tell based on different cultures.
D. Extensive reading time.

Answer: A. Wait time.
Answer B, C, and D can all be discounted since they are standard practice for language arts teachers. Answer A the amount of time a teacher waits for an answer from her students can be very difficult to change. Teachers may be somewhat impatient ('Let's get on with it'), lack understanding ('If they knew the answer, they would respond'), and unaware of differences between the U.S. and other cultures. Answer A is the correct response.

67. Community Language Learning requires the members of the group and the teacher to:
(Rigorous)

A. Use cue cards and pictures.
B. Trust each other.
C. Use self-expression to expand their knowledge.
D. React physically to a command

Answer: C. A language learning strategy.
The cards and pictures were used in the audio-lingual method. The Silent Way is based on student's use of self-expression to expand their knowledge. TPR expects students to react physically and carry out commands. The Community Language Learning method emphasizes teacher-student trust and approaching learning as a dynamic and creative process.

68. **If the teacher circulates around the room answering questions and asking others, she is demonstrating which level(s) of scaffolding:** *(Rigorous)*

A. Modeling.
B. Interactive.
C. Guided.
D. Independent.

Answer: B. Interactive; C. Guided.
If the teacher were modeling, she would be demonstrating correct pronunciation or syntax to the students. If the ELLs were at an independent level, they would not need scaffolding. By circulating and answering questions, she can be interactive and guide the learning— possibly through asking other questions.

69. **Ms. Mejia is concerned that her ELLs learn to write correctly in English. She:** *(Average)*

A. Dictates sentences with the week's spelling words.
B. Plays Hangman to reinforce spelling of the words.
C. Reads stories using vocabulary the ELLs need for BICS or CALP.
D. Sends extra work home for the ELLs to practice.

Answer: C. Reads stories using vocabulary the ELLs need for BICS or CALP.
Dictation is a good strategy if the words are in context. Hangman is a fun game and good for spelling, but little else. Extra work home for the ELLs in writing would probably not improve their writing skills, but continue the same errors. The best option is C to provide ELLs with the vocabulary they need for BICS and CALP. By modeling the language the ELLs need in contexts, they should be able to acquire it.

70. Angela needs help in English. Her teacher suggested several things Angela can do to improve her learning strategies. One of the following is <u>not</u> a socioaffective learning strategy.
    (Easy)

    A. Read a funny book.
    B. Work cooperatively with her classmates.
    C. Ask the teacher to speak more slowly.
    D. Skim for information.

    Answer: D. Skim for information.
    Options A, B and C are all socioaffective learning strategies. Answer D is a cognitive strategy and the correct choice.

71. An ESOL teacher who encourages her students to keep track of their progress in English Language Learning is stimulating which learning strategy?
    (Rigorous)

    A. Metacognitive
    B. Affective
    C. Cognitive
    D. Social

    Answer: A. Metacognitive.
    This ESOL teacher is instructing her ELLs in strategies that make them aware of their individual learning. By being aware of their learning strategies, ELLs can compare their previous learning with their actual learning and measure their progress (or lack of).

72. Advanced TPR might include:
    (Average)

    A. Rapid fire commands.
    B. More advanced vocabulary.
    C. Funny commands.
    D. All of the above.

    Answer: D. All of the above.
    Total Physical Response can be done slowly as a beginning activity for ELLs. As they begin to understand more oral English and the game, TPR can be 'spiced up' by all of the suggestions.

73. Which of the following is <u>not</u> a step in the Language Experience Approach?
(Rigorous)

A. Students draw a picture to represent something personal about an experience.
B. Students dictate their story to the teacher.
C. The teacher reads the story revising where necessary.
D. The story is read in later days as a follow-up activity.

Answer: C. The teacher reads the story revising where necessary.
In the Language Experience Approach, the teacher writes the revised sentences on the storyboard making the necessary corrections at this time.

74. Content-based instruction suggests LEP students need an additional 5-7 years to pick-up academic language. During this time period, content area teachers should <u>not</u>:

(Average)

A. Correct the LEP's oral language mistakes.

B. Speak more slowly, enunciation.

C. Demonstrate new materials using various strategies to increase input.

D. Check frequently for comprehension by asking students to explain what was said to a classmate or back to the teacher.

Answer: A. Correct the LEP's oral language mistakes.
A far more effective method is to correct the LEP's mistakes when working on written work because there is a visual record of the mistake.

75. The researcher most identified with the importance of working through problems to obtain a solution and to learn a foreign language is:
(Rigorous)

   A. Asher.

   B. Krashen & Terrell.

   C. Postovsky.

   D. Prabhu.

Answer: D. Prabhu.
Asher's work was based on Total Physical Response (TPR) as a comprehension-based approach (CBA). Krashen & Terrell theorized about Second Language Acquisition. Postovsky's work concerned a CBA/CBL-based approach involving computers and problem-solving tasks. Prabhu researched the effectiveness of problem solving as a means of students acquiring the language they needed to learn English versus the learning of the language in order to solve problems. His students used information-gap activities, reasoning activities, and opinion-gap activities to acquire the new language they needed.

76. Which of the following instructional approaches emphasizes LEPs working on content?
(Average)

   A. TPR.

   B. The Natural Approach.

   C. CALLA.

   D. The Communicative Approach.

Answer: C. CALLA.
CALLA is the brain-child of Chamot and O'Malley. Their work is based on the principle that the child learns far more language in content classes than in ESOL pull-out classes. CALLA (Cognitive Academic Language Learning Approach) integrates language development, content area instruction and explicit instruction in learning strategies.

77. **The Schema Theory of Carrell & Eisterhold suggests that for learning to take place, teachers must:**
(Rigorous)

A. Integrate content areas with ESOL techniques.

B. Emphasize all four language skills.

C. Present comprehensible input in a meaningful context.

D. Relate new materials to previous knowledge.

Answer: D. Relate new materials to previous knowledge.
The schema theory of Carrell & Eisterhold suggests that schema must be related to previous knowledge or learning does not take place. When activated, schema are able to evaluate the new materials in light of previous knowledge. If the arguments made convincing to the learner, he or she accepts them and integrates the new knowledge in to his data bank. Otherwise, the new materials are unconvincing, the new knowledge rejected by the learner.

78. **According to Cummins four levels of difficulty, the high school math teacher whose ELLs work on standard workbook problems, is using _____ materials.**
(Average)

A. Level 1: Cognitively undemanding / Context-embedded

B. Level 2: Cognitively undemanding / Context-reduced

C. Level 3: Cognitively demanding / Context-embedded

D. Level 4: Cognitively demanding / Context-reduced

Answer: D. Level 4: Cognitively demanding / Context-reduced. Math materials in high school are cognitively demanding, but standard workbook activities are not related to a context the ELLs know—their school, their community, or their families and are therefore, context-reduced.

79. **Identify one of the following methods of dealing with fossilization as not appropriate.**
(Average)

A. Ignore mistakes that do not interfere with meaning.

B. Work on items such as ending /s/ for third person singular in written work.

C. Teacher (or aide) corrects all the errors in the papers.

D. Dictating correct sentences of patterns frequently used incorrectly by ELLs.

Answer: C. Teacher (or aide) corrects all the errors in the papers.
Peer correction is an effective way of dealing with fossilization. Both the ELL and his or her peer have the opportunity to analyze errors in a non-confrontational way.

80. **Identify one method of adapting general education instruction to ELLs.**
(Average)

A. Providing extra listening materials (e.g. CD-Rom's of stories).

B. Arrange homogenous work groups.

C. Using an English dictionary.

D. Using grade-level storybooks.

Answer: A. Providing extra listening materials (e.g. CD-Rom's of stories).
By providing extra listening materials to the ELLs, they are receiving scaffolding. Since the CD-Rom's provide modeling of correct pronunciation and stress, the ELLs are receiving English language instruction at the same time as they are receiving additional help in understanding the story.

81. Using a 'video split':
(Rigorous)

A. Is effective with science experiments.

B. Is an information gap activity.

C. Forces ELLs to use L2.

D. Creates awareness of authentic language.

Answer: B. Is an information gap activity.
Information gap activities are activities in which certain information is revealed to the different groups. A video split might typically allow one group to see the video without sound and the other group to hear the sound without the visuals. They would share the information they received in order to complete the task.

82. When using instructional technology (e.g. videos, DVDs, or CDs) in ESOL classes, the instructor should:
(Rigorous)

A. Play the entire piece to build listening skills.

B. Frequently stop to check on comprehension.

C. Quiz the ELLs for comprehension after listening.

D. Block the captions on the video.

Answer: B. Frequently stop to check on comprehension.
Answer A: play the entire piece to build listening skills would be tiring and boring for most ELLs. Listening for long periods of time before they are ready causes most language learners to 'tune out'. Answer C would raise the affective filter and lessen language learning. Answer D omits a source of visual information for the ELLs. Answer D is the correct option as the teacher can stop the video and check to see that everyone understands. This will maintain motivation and increase interest in the activity.

83. Using asynchronous applications teachers can:
(Average)

A. Design coursework for students to complete by specific dates.

B. Send instant messages (IMs).

C. Enhance student interaction.

D. Increase student's interest.

Answer: A. Design coursework for students to complete by specific dates.
Asynchronous applications are applications off-line. As such, the teacher can script a course completely at the teacher's convenience and programmed to be available on a specific date of the teacher's choice. Once completed, they may be used over and over.

84. **CALL gives ELLs the opportunity to:**
(Rigorous)

A. Practice writing skills in chatrooms.

B. Receive instructor feedback during the class.

C. See each other through video conferencing.

D. All of the above.

Answer: D. All of the above.

85. **Kroonenberg believes the value of CMC:**
(Rigorous)

A. For instructors, is that they can integrate video and audio into instruction.

B. Is that its authoring software tools help teachers prepare course materials.

C. Lies in its ability to imitate live conversation.

D. Is achieved by cultural authenticity.

Answer: D. Level 4: Cognitively demanding / Context-reduced.
Computer-mediated communication simulates a live conversation and is the best choice.

86. **Teachers looking for reading comprehension software for young ELLs should look for:**
(Average)

A. Illustrated vocabulary lists, which are presented before the story.

B. A text which is read accompanied by animation.

C. Interactive vocabulary words.

D. A page for the students to illustrate their retelling of the story at the end.

Answer: B. A text which is read accompanied by animation.
Vocabulary lists and vocabulary words will help the student understand more, but do not work on comprehension of the story. The painting activity would be a concluding activity and not necessarily based on understanding the story. The best option is B because the animation attracts the young child visually. Having a story read to the child helps with pre-literacy skills especially comprehension where much of our understanding may come from hearing the words pronounced that we see.

87. The most appropriate ESOL strategy for readers who do not read in their L1 is to:
(Average)

A. Postpone reading until the ELLs acquire intermediate oral language proficiency.

B. Teach cognates and high frequency words.

C. Develop literacy in L1 first.

D. Use pull-out reading support in L2.

Answer: C. Develop literacy in L1 first.
Once the ELL understands pre-reading strategies and how the written word is connected to the spoken word, the learner is ready to read. Once fluency is achieved in the first language, second language reading instruction can begin and be more successful.

88. ELLs who are beginning to write in L2 demonstrate which traits:
(Average)

A. Word-order problems, lack of variety in vocabulary, use different sentence patterns.

B. Write 3 or more paragraphs with run-on sentences, little vocabulary above basic level, limited organization.

C. Limited vocabulary, use one or two sentence patterns, write only a few sentences.

D. Ask for translation of vocabulary at times, good variety of sentence patterns, write a paragraph or more.

Answer: C. Limited vocabulary, uses one or two sentence patterns, writes only a few sentences.
ELLs often demonstrate mixed traits in their writing skills. Answer C is the best option because all of the traits mentioned are at a beginning level.

89. All of the following strategies except one are recommended to promote emergent literacy. It is:
(Average)

A. Teacher reads oversized books carefully pointing to each word as she reads.

B. Mother Goose rhymes illustrated around the room.

C. Spelling lists for homework practice.

D. Word wall with words listed under each beginning letter.

Answer: C. Spelling lists for homework practice.
Spelling lists are out of context and not recommended to promote literacy. Any word list, if given, must be in the context of the classroom learning.

90. **Incorporating prior knowledge into L2 learning does not:**
(Average)

A. Permit readers to learn and remember more.
B. Cause poor readers.
C. Help readers to evaluate new arguments.
D. Improve comprehension.

Answer: B. Cause poor readers.
Activating schema and incorporating previous knowledge into L2 learning will strengthen the learning process. It certainly does not cause poor readers.

91. **Freire's research states:**
(Average)

A. Critical literacy provides a means for individual to identify with the nature of social conditions and change them.

B. Critical literacy is an investigation into the motives and goals of an author or speaker.

C. Readers are critical consumers of information received.

D. Oppressed people obtain power through education and knowledge.

Answer: D. Oppressed people obtain power through education and knowledge.
Various authors (Auerbach 1999; Brown, 1999; Hammond & Macken Horaik, 1999 and Hull, 2000) have stated that critical literacy provides individuals with a means to identify with and change social conditions. Lohrey (1998) spoke of critical literacy as an investigation into the motives and goals of an author. Van Duzer & Florez (2000) asserted that critical literacy goes beyond the basic literacy skills and asks readers to become critical consumers of information. Freire's assertion was that oppressed people obtain power through education and knowledge.

92. An English teacher included a unit on Shakespeare's Romeo and Juliet in her programming. To promote critical literacy, she could have her students:
(Average)

A. Provide a list of pre-reading questions for discussion.
B. Use a flow-chart to outline the plot.
C. Compare the story of Prince Charles and Princess Diana to Romeo and Juliet.
D. Show the movie and provide comprehension questions.

Answer: C. Compare the story of Prince Charles and Princess Diana to Romeo and Juliet.
Answer A would activate previous knowledge and create interest in the story. Option B suggests a flow-chart could be used as a plot summary. Option D provides extra input for better understanding of the story. Only answer C is giving the students opportunities for critical analysis and a means of exploring universal themes in family relationships with a meaningful context of the modern world.

93. Instruction to promote fluency includes:
(Average)

A. Developing writing and reading skills separately.
B. Explicit study of vocabulary lists.
C. Role plays, phonics instruction, journal writing.
D. Learning only the specific language for the task at hand.

Answer: C. Role plays, phonics instruction, journal writing.
Answers A, B, and D may be discarded as options since they are all poor ESOL techniques. Only Answer C suggests various ways in which fluency is developed by constant practice in non-threatening ways.

94. Young children are often considered better language learners than older children or adults. However, older children or adults may be able to progress more rapidly in reading instruction because: *(Rigorous)*

    A. They have more worldly experience to help them understand the texts.

    B. Their vocabulary concepts in L2 are less developed.

    C. They have more language learning experience.

    D. Phonics is the same whether in L1 or L2.

Answer: A. They have more worldly experience to help them understand texts.
Answers B and C would depend on the individuals involved in the learning situation. Answer D can readily be discarded as sounds are what distinguish many languages one from another. The correct answer is A. Older learners can apply their worldly experience and schema developed in L1 to understanding L2 texts as well as other language learning situations.

95. Teachers of ELL students should be able to use both verbal and non-verbal communication techniques. Identify each of the following as Verbal (V) or Non-verbal Speech (NV).
(Average)

    A. _____ Mime

    B. _____ Initiating

    C. _____ Paraphrasing

    D. _____ Gestures

    E. _____ Summarizing

    F. _____ Acting out a sequence of events

    G. _____ Questioning

    H. _____ Listening

Answers: A-NV, B-V, C-V, D-NV, E-V, F-NV, G-V, H-V.

96. **Technology and globalization have placed increased demands on schools. One disappointment of ELL education has been:**
(Rigorous)

A. ELLs often succeed in the corporate ranks.
B. Bilingual skills are in great demand.
C. Too many ELLs make little use of their language skills.
D. ELLs frequently return to their native lands.

Answer: C. Too many ELLs make little use of their language skills.
Many factors enter into the politics of L2 learning. One disappointment ahs be the inability of low-achieving students to graduate from high school, enter college, and graduate. Their place in the workforce has too often seen ELLs accepting low paying or low skilled jobs that do not take advantage of their language skills.

97. **Culture and cultural differences:**
(Average)

A. Must be addressed by the teacher in the ELL classroom by pointing out cultural similarities and differences.
B. Should be the starting point for learning about how culture affects the ELLs attitude towards education.
C. Positively affects how well ELLs perform in the language classroom.
D. May have strong emotional influence on the ELL learner.

Answer: D. May have strong emotional influence on the ELL learner.
Culture and cultural differences may be addressed by the skillful ESOL teacher, but frequently teachers are unaware of all the cultures and cultural differences they are dealing with. At the same time, it may be possible to determine how his or her culture affects the ELL's attitude towards education; however, it may well be something the young child cannot express or the adult hides for various reasons. Culture and cultural differences does not always play a positive role in the learning process. Culture and cultural differences may have a strong emotional influence on the ELL learner frequently the case whether it be negative or positive. Thus, D is our best option.

98. Pierre arrived in the U. S. in 2005. He has been living with his uncle and aunt who are well assimilated into the U.S. culture. Pierre misses his parents and brothers. He finds his high school studies fairly easy and his classmates lazy. He is worried about his goal of becoming a professional soccer player and doesn't understand why he can't have wine with his meals when he eats out with his aunt and uncle. In which stage of assimilation is Pierre?
(Average)

A. Honeymoon stage.
B. Hostility stage.
C. Humor stage.
D. Home stage.

Answer: B. Hostility stage.
While Pierre is probably adapting, he still finds his culture superior ('his classmates are lazy' and 'why he can't have wine with his meal') and the new culture deficient ('worried about his goal of becoming a professional soccer player').

99. Upon arrival in a new country, immigrants frequently show signs of _____ in order to get a job.
(Easy)

A. Assimilation.
B. Acculturation.
C. Transculturation.
D. Accommodation.

Answer: D. Accommodation.
While new immigrants acquire the skills they need to succeed in their new culture, they may accommodate their cultural heritage to the new one. Later as they are more fully integrated into the host society, they may begin to feel less intimidated and demonstrate their heritage culture more openly.

100. **Which of the following accommodations may be allowed for ELLs during assessment?**
(Average)

A. Giving extra time.
B. Asking proctor to explain certain words or test items.
C. Paraphrasing the prompt.
D. May use an English-heritage translating dictionary.

Answer: D. May use an English-heritage dictionary.
Answers A, B, and C would defeat the purpose of assessing the ELLs. Answer D is the appropriate accommodation during assessment.

101. **Which of the following is <u>not</u> an acceptable alternative assessment strategy for ELLs?**
(Average)

A. Portfolios.

B. Observation.

C. Self-assessment.

D. Essay writing.

Answer: D. Essay writing.
Answer D is the correct response as essay writing is not an appropriate strategy for evaluating the English capabilities of ELLs.

102. **Which method is the most appropriate method for dealing partially with cultural bias in tests?**
(Rigorous)

A. Translate the tests previous to the actual exam.

B. Provide pictures and graphics during the test.

C. Administer practice tests with time limits.

D. Provide a study guide and give test orally.

Answer: C. Administer practice tests with time limits.
Answers A, B, and D are accommodations to the language deficiencies of ELLs, but do not address cultural bias. Answer C addresses cultural bias since many cultures do not time tests and ELLs may find this a difficulty since it is a norm in many U.S. testing environments.

103. **When testing for an ELLs level of English proficiency, which minor accommodation is appropriate?**
(Rigorous)

    A. Extra time may be allowed.

    B. Using the ELLs portfolio.

    C. Recitation.

    D. Providing translation of prompts as needed for understanding.

    Answer: A. Extra time may be allowed.
    Answers B and C suggest alternative testing methods. Answer D is inappropriate as the level of English proficiency is being tested. Answer A is the correct answer as ELLs may need more time to respond to questions until they become more familiar with the English language and U.S. testing situations.

104. **Before coming to the U.S., Sven, an 11-grade student took the TOEFL. This is a _____ test.**
(Easy)

    A. Language proficiency.

    B. Language achievement.

    C. Language placement.

    D. Diagnostic language.

    Answer: A. Language proficiency.
    Since the TOEFL tests a student's English language ability in reading comprehension, essay writing, syntax and lexis, it tests for language proficiency.

105. A 5th grader has completed one year in the ESOL program but does not seem to make progress. Which of the following might indicate a learning disability?
(Rigorous)

    A. Frequently code switches.

    B. Needs extra time to answer questions.

    C. Is able to decode successfully but has comprehension difficulties.

    D. Dropping of the final consonants of words.

Answer: C. Is able to decode successfully but has comprehension difficulties.
Answers A and B are normal ELL reactions to the stress of learning a new language. Answer D refers to a pronunciation error which may be normal in the ELL's first language. Only C goes beyond the normal problems of ESOL and possibly into the realm of learning difficulties.

106. An ELL student may pronounce /free/ instead of /three/. This is an example of:
(Rigorous)

    A. Omission.

    B. Substitution.

    C. Distortion.

    D. Addition.

Answer: C. Distortion.
In distortion, the ELL pronounces the phoneme incorrectly and 'distorts' the sound.

107. Which of the following is indicative of a language disorder rather than a L2 developmental issue?
(Rigorous)

    A. Difficulty in identifying words in context.

    B. Inability to produce grammatically correct sentences.

    C. Dropping of specific word endings.

    D. Speech is difficult for others to understand.

Answer: D. Speech is difficult for others to understand.
Answers A, B, and C are all problems in ELLs. Only Answer D would not be considered a problem of L2 learners. Therefore, it may indicate a language disorder.

108. **Which of the following should be done prior to initiating a formal referral process for an ELL with possible learning disabilities?** *(Rigorous)*

    A. A vision and hearing test.

    B. A language diagnostic test.

    C. Documentation of at least 1 intervention.

    D. Consultation with principal about ELL's progress.

    Answer: A. A vision and hearing test.
    Answer A is the correct selection since it eliminates the possibility of a childhood health issue before classifying it as a learning disorder problem.

109. **Which of the following is a possible sign of the gifted ELL student?** *(Average)*

    A. Normal development according to parental interview.

    B. Speech delayed in L2.

    C. Seems to solve logic problems with difficulty.

    D. High academic performance in L1.

    Answer: D. High academic performance in L1.
    Answer D suggests that ELLs who performed excellent academic work in their first language would be the prime indicator of a student with exceptional abilities, especially if they are apparent in the L2 also.

110. **An ELL suspected of having learning difficulties:** (Rigorous)

    A. May present behavioral differences when asked to produce written work.

B. Might demonstrate the ability to learn quickly.

C. Should be analyzed for up to 10 weeks using ESOL techniques.

D. May demonstrate the ability to solve problems not dependent on English.

Answer: D. Skim for information.
Answers B and D indicate ability beyond the realm of language learning difficulties; they suggest gifted exceptionalities. Answer A suggest the ELL may be acting out to avoid producing work that is challenging or too difficult. The correct answer would be C which indicates carefully documented follow-up to avoid placing an ELL in the incorrect environment.

111. **Identify the correct order for assessment of ELLs with exceptionalities.**
     (Rigorous)

    A. English language assessment, language proficiency assessment, language for assessment.

    B. Speech and language assessment, language for assessment, English language assessment.

    C. Language for assessment, speech and language assessment, language proficiency.

    D. Language proficiency assessment, speech and language assessment, English language assessment.

    Answer: B. Language proficiency assessment, speech and language
    assessment, English language assessment.
    Answer B reflects the correct order of assessment.

112. **Which of the following instructional strategies would <u>not</u> be appropriate for ELLs with exceptionalities?**
     (Rigorous

    A. Use of texts adapted to students disability.

    B. Practice testing opportunities.

    C. Differentiated instruction.

    D. Lectures.

    Answer: D. Lectures.
    Answer D is the correct one. Lectures are difficult for most people and certainly for ELLs whose attention span may be limited by their exceptionality and their L2 language proficiency level.

113. In a school where numerous ELL students of the same language group are present, the most efficient way to ensure conformity with the Consent Decree may be:
(Rigorous)

   A. Pull-out classes for science and math

   B. Mainstream content instruction with pull-out for Language Arts instruction.

   C. Mainstream instruction for Language Arts, science and math with tutorials in problem areas.

   D. Pull-out classes for Language Arts and science, mainstream for math.

Answer: D. Pull-out classes for Language Arts and science, mainstream for math.
In many cases, where students come to the U.S. with previous schooling, it is considered unnecessary, and indeed undesirable, for students to be pulled-out for math classes since math symbols are usually universal. Therefore, students will probably benefit more from remaining in the regular math classroom.

114. The No Child Left Behind Act established:
(Rigorous)

   A. Title I funds are available only if the schools participate in National Assessment of Education Progress.

   B. Bilingual programs must be effective and established three criteria.

   C. High performance children cannot be used to average out low performing ELLs.

   D. Schools must form and convene assessment committees.

Answer: C. High performance children cannot be used to average out low performing ELLs.
Selection A refers to the establishment of voluntary school participation in NAEP after the National Committee on Excellence in Education produced their report **A Nation at Risk** (1983). Selection B refers to the decision rendered in Castaneda v Pickard (1981). One requirement resulting from Lau v Nichols (1974) was that schools must form and

convene assessment committees. The NCLB act specifically states that disaggregated data must be used in evaluating school performance.

115. *Bilingual Schooling and the Miami Experience* documents Miami-Dade County's:
(*Easy*)

A. Experience in scaffolding.

B. As pioneers in ESL in the U.S.

C. As leading investigators in EFL in the U.S.

D. Reaction to cultural differences.

Answer: B. Pioneers in ESL in the U. S.
Bilingual Schooling and the Miami Experience is a re-issue of *Bilingual School for a Bicultural Community: Miami's Adaptation to the Cuban Refugees*. It documents the experiences of Miami-Dade County in reaction to the increased demands placed on the school system from 1959 up until 1973 when there was a wave of Cuban immigrants. There is a new introduction providing information on more recent immigration from Cuba, the Caribbean as well as Central and South America.

116. **In schools with large immigrant populations of diverse origin, the most commonly used model is:**
(*Average*)

A. Submersion.

B. Pull-out ESL.

C. SDAIE.

D. Transition.

Answer: B. Pull-out model.
SDAIE or Specially Designed Academic Programs in English is structured immersion model most commonly used in California. The submersion model does not provide the necessary support that ELLs need and is in disfavor. Transition models provided approximately three years of BICS but frequently leave the LEP with almost no support while learning CALP. Today, the most commonly used model is B: Pull-out ESL.

117. **Widdowson's definition of 'use' and 'usage' is well demonstrated in which of the following models?**
(Rigorous)

   A. Canadian French Immersion and Miami-Dade Count models

   B. Submersion with primary language support

   C. Content-based ESL and indigenous language immersion

   D. Communication-based ESL and Grammar-based ESL.

   Answer: D. Communication-based ESL and Grammar-based ESL.
   The question refers to Answer D. Widdowson differentiated between how the grammar of a language is reflected in its 'usage' and a languages' actual 'use' in communicative situations.

118. **Based on Title III of the No Child Left Behind Act, schools are required to include ELLs in state-mandated testing:**
(Rigorous)

   A. In mathematics and science after 2 years of enrollment.

   B. In English language arts, math, and science after 2 years enrollment.

   C. In English language arts and math after enrollment.

   D. In mathematics with 1 year of enrollment.

   Answer: D. In mathematics with 1 year of enrollment.

119. **The No Child Left Behind Act requires schools to:**
(Rigorous)

   A. Give assessment in English if the LEP has received 3 years of schooling in the US (except for Puerto Rico).

   B. Measure school districts by status.

   C. Inform parents of the school's evaluation.

   D. Includes LEPs in all academic assessments.

   Answer: A. Give assessment in English if the LEP has received 3 years of schooling in the U.S. (except for Puerto Rico).

Since NCLB requires schools to focus on quality education for students who were often overlooked by the educational system, in general, LEPs with three years of schooling must be tested in English.

120. In Lau v Nichols (1974), the Supreme Court ruled that:
(Rigorous)

A. School districts may not continue education programs that fail to produce positive results for ELLs.

B. Prohibited sexual harassment in any school activity on or off campus.

C. Students were denied an 'equal' education.

D. Prohibited discrimination against students and employers based on race, ethnicity, national origins, disability, or marital status.

Answer: C. Students were denied and 'equal' education.
Answer A refers to Castaneda v Pickard (1981). Answer B refers to Title IX of the Education Amendments of 1972. Answer D was covered in Florida Educational Equity Act of 1984. Only Option C refers to Lau v Nichols (1974).

XAMonline, INC. 25 First St. Suite 106 Cambridge MA 02141

Toll Free number 800-509-4128

TO ORDER Fax 781-662-9268 OR www.XAMonline.com

NEW YORK STATE TEACHER CERTIFICATION EXAMINATION - NYSTCE - 2009

PO#   Store/School:

Address 1:

Address 2 (Ship to other):

City, State Zip

Credit card number_____-_____-_____-_____   expiration_____

EMAIL _____

PHONE   FAX

ISBN	TITLE	Qty	Retail	Total
978-1-60787-155-2	NYSTCE ATS-W Assessment of Teaching Skills-Written 090, 091		$29.95	
978-1-58197-260-3	NYSTCE ATAS ASSESSMENT OF TEACHING ASSISTANT SKILLS 095		$59.95	
978-1-58197-289-4	CST BIOLOGY 006		$59.95	
978-1-58197-769-1	CST CHEMISTRY 007		$59.95	
978-1-58197-865-0	CQST COMMUNICATION AND QUANTITATIVE SKILLS TEST 080		$17.95	
978-1-58197-632-8	CST EARTH SCIENCE 008		$59.95	
978-1-58197-267-2	CST ENGLISH 003		$59.95	
978-1-58197-858-2	CST FRENCH SAMPLE TEST 012		$15.00	
978-1-58197-344-0	LAST LIBERAL ARTS AND SCIENCE TEST 001		$16.95	
978-1-58197-863-6	CST LIBRARY MEDIA SPECIALIST 074		$59.95	
978-1-58197-623-6	CST LITERACY 065		$59.95	
978-1-60787-154-5	CST MATH 004		$34.95	
978-1-58197-290-0	CST MUTIPLE SUBJECTS 002		$28.95	
978-1-58197-579-6	CST PHYSICAL EDUCATION 076		$59.95	
978-1-58197-042-5	CST PHYSICS 009		$59.95	
978-1-58197-265-8	CST SOCIAL STUDIES 005		$59.95	
978-1-58197-396-9	CST SPANISH 020		$59.95	
978-1-58197-258-0	CST STUDENTS WITH DISABILITIES 060		$73.50	
978-1-60787-153-8	NYSTCE English to Speakers of Other Languages 022		$59.95	
			SUBTOTAL	
Shipping	1 book $8.70, 2 books $11.00, 3+ books $15.00		Ship	
			TOTAL	